13 Days in Ferguson

★

13 DAYS IN FERGUSON

CAPTAIN RONALD JOHNSON
with ALAN EISENSTOCK

TYNDALE
MOMENTUM®

The nonfiction imprint of
Tyndale House Publishers, Inc.

Visit Tyndale online at www.tyndale.com.

Visit Tyndale Momentum online at www.tyndalemomentum.com.

TYNDALE, *Tyndale Momentum*, and Tyndale's quill logo are registered trademarks of Tyndale House Publishers, Inc. The Tyndale Momentum logo is a trademark of Tyndale House Publishers, Inc. Tyndale Momentum is the nonfiction imprint of Tyndale House Publishers, Inc., Carol Stream, Illinois.

13 Days in Ferguson

Designed by Dean H. Renninger

Edited by Dave Lindstedt

For information about special discounts for bulk purchases, please contact Tyndale House Publishers at csresponse@tyndale.com, or call 1-800-323-9400.

ISBN 978-1-4964-1657-5

Printed in the United States of America

24	23	22	21	20	19	18
7	6	5	4	3	2	1

To all the men and women in Ferguson
on both sides, on all sides, who stood for humanity,
for change, and for freedom

~and~

To Sister Mary Antona Ebo
(Franciscan Sister of Mary)
Your blessed memory and angelic spirit
will live within me forever.

CONTENTS

PROLOGUE

TWO MONTHS AFTER FERGUSON

CONFRONTATION

In short, we, the black and the white, deeply
need each other here if we are really to become a
nation—if we are really, that is, to achieve our
identity, our maturity, as men and women.

JAMES BALDWIN
THE FIRE NEXT TIME

THEY SIT A COUPLE OF TABLES AWAY, staring at me.

Four of them. Well muscled, steely eyed, rural Midwestern, midtwenties to early thirties. White. Two with shaved heads, two with military buzz cuts. All four in full camouflage and jackboots. Laughing too loud, pounding beers, chewing tobacco, drawing attention to themselves.

I keep them locked in my periphery. One of them senses me eyeing him and nods slowly. I'd call the look menacing.

I turn away, sigh, and speak as quietly as I can to my daughter and her boyfriend.

"Don't look, but across from us, a couple of tables down, we have four gentlemen who have been staring at me this whole time."

I wait a beat while Amanda glances over. When she turns back, her eyes narrow and she shakes her head, not understanding.

"Things happened," I say. "People didn't always agree with me. I knew at some point I would be confronted in public." I cock my head, smile, and try to appear calm. "Tonight's the night."

"What do we do?"

"I want you guys to walk out the door. If anything happens—" I catch myself. "Don't worry. I'll be okay."

Amanda's eyes widen slightly, sparkle. "Maybe I should call Mom."

I laugh. I'm a twenty-seven-year veteran of the Missouri State Highway Patrol; I go six two, two forty; and my daughter's telling me to call my wife. She has a way of defusing even the most difficult situations.

I gently squeeze Amanda's hand, and she doesn't argue. Gathering her purse, cell phone, and scarf, and with a minimum of clatter and scraping of chairs, she and her boyfriend exit the sports bar.

I sip my Pepsi and wait. For a fleeting second, I consider calling for backup, but I immediately dismiss the thought. I'm in this alone. This confrontation is about me, my actions, my decisions—and, I expect, about both the color of my uniform and the color of my skin.

Adrenaline revving, I signal the waitress for the check. She holds up a finger, and after clearing some dishes from another table, arrives at my side with her hands shoved into the pockets of her uniform.

"All taken care of," she says.

I stare at her for what must be a solid ten seconds, and she starts to laugh.

"Somebody paid your bill."

"Really? Who?"

She shrugs. "The party wants to remain anonymous."

I scan the entire restaurant. I don't recognize anyone. Nobody makes eye contact with me. I look up at the waitress.

"Come on, tell me."

She pokes her finger out of her pocket and subtly points behind her. I follow the direction of her fingernail and search every face in the vicinity, but I can't for the life of me identify anyone who would have picked up my check.

"I don't see where you're pointing," I say.

She rolls her eyes, tightens her lips, and speaks like a ventriloquist: "The four guys over there."

"Those guys?"

I don't remember getting to my feet or walking over, but I find myself standing at their table. They pause their conversation and look up at me.

"I'm sorry to interrupt your dinner," I say. "I just wanted to thank you for paying my bill."

One of the guys smiles and looks away. Another one taps his fingers on the table.

"You're welcome," he says.

"But why?"

"We live here," the finger tapper says. "We appreciate what you've done."

"Thank you," I say again. "Sincerely."

Then, one by one, I shake their hands.

I return to my table, pick up my cell phone, and head toward the exit. Halfway to the door, I stop and look back at the four guys who bought dinner for my daughter, her boyfriend, and me. Four young white guys with shaved heads, dressed in full camouflage and jackboots, laughing too loud and pounding beers. The last guys I ever would have expected.

I feel embarrassed. And I feel small.

I've had the confrontation I expected. What I didn't expect was that the confrontation would be between myself and my own bias. I experienced firsthand how easily and suddenly we can cross over into presumption and even paranoia.

We're all biased in some way, every one of us. It's what we do with our bias that matters. We can't allow it to affect our attitudes, influence our decisions, or inform our behavior. Instead, we must acknowledge it. We must be humbled by it. Ignoring our biases or believing they are *truth*—and refusing to change when we recognize bias within ourselves—that's when bias becomes bigotry and prejudice becomes racism.

How do we overcome these tendencies that so often seem to separate people in our nation from one another?

Admitting that we all have our biases seems like a good place to start.

DAY 1

SATURDAY, AUGUST 9, 2014

MICHAEL BROWN'S BODY

Please, God, let me be enough.
I just want to be enough.

RON JOHNSON

THE FIRST CALL COMES IN around one o'clock in the afternoon. I'm in a car with three other African American state troopers, returning from a National Black State Troopers Coalition conference in Milwaukee. My cell phone vibrates, and I take the call. A lieutenant from our office reports that there has been an officer-involved shooting of a young black man in Ferguson and a crowd has begun to gather.

"Ferguson," I say.

Anywhere, USA.

A town like so many others.

I basically grew up in Ferguson. Half the kids in Ferguson go to Riverview Gardens High, the same high school I attended. I played football there, ran track, played in the marching band, went to prom, walked in my graduation.

An officer-involved shooting.

Crowds gathering.

Unrest developing.

In *Ferguson?*

I can't wrap my head around this. We're not talking about a depressed, dangerous, potential powder keg like the south side of Chicago or St. Louis City, where I once lived. Ferguson has its share of challenges and problems—poverty, crime—but nothing you could point to that would precipitate an officer-involved shooting.

At least that's what I thought.

"Keep me updated," I tell the lieutenant. I click off my cell and pass along the news to the other officers.

Several hours later, the lieutenant calls again.

"Things have escalated," he says. He explains that more people have flooded the residential street in Ferguson where the shooting took place. He also tells me in a low monotone that the body has not yet been removed from the street, now nearly four hours after the shooting.

"This could turn into something bad," I say.

When the lieutenant informs me that many more officers have reported to the scene, I end the call and tell the other troopers about the crowd escalation and the body still lying in the street.

We all go silent. For a moment, I shut off the thoughts that are spinning in my mind and focus only on the sounds I hear— the rumble of the car on the road, a sigh, an intake of breath, a throat clearing. But a moment later, the images of race riots from fifty years ago come charging unchecked into my mind's eye—buildings burning; black men being beaten and shot, their bodies left on the streets, their heads pressed against curbs, their faces in the gutters. Pictures of hatred. Reminders. Examples. Warnings.

Another time, I tell myself. *Another place.*

"They still haven't removed the body?" someone asks.

"Four hours," another trooper says. "In the *street*."

"If that were *my* child—"

An intake of breath.

A sigh.

A throat clearing.

The rumble of the car on the road.

★

At home, six hours later, I watch the news with my wife, Lori. While the local reporters at the scene relay the latest information, behind them and around them the crowds gather and swirl—people's anger, frustration, and outrage simmering, threatening to boil over.

I lower the volume on the television as my phone rings with updates, the news dribbling in, though many details remain vague or unconfirmed.

Outside contractors working for a funeral parlor have finally removed Michael Brown's body.

Reportedly, a robbery was committed.

Michael Brown was apparently unarmed.

The police officer, the shooter—name withheld—is Caucasian.

Protesters are mobilizing; the police presence is growing.

My training kicks in, and my mind begins a makeshift checklist. Based on the rules in our officer training manual for crowd control, the goal is to secure the area and make the streets safe.

On TV, a newscaster stands in front of a mound of rubble

near the site of the shooting, describing what, only a short time ago, had been a growing memorial to Michael Brown—flowers, photos, candles, cards, stuffed animals. According to reports, he says, a police officer allowed a dog on a leash to urinate on the memorial and then another officer drove a police vehicle over the memorial and destroyed it.

I have no words. I look over at my wife as her eyes water with confusion and pain.

Why is this happening?

I turn back to the news.

Ferguson.

A place I thought I knew.

Suddenly I don't know where I am.

★

Lying in bed, my eyes jacked open, my body rigid, my arms glued to my sides beneath a single white sheet, I hear the central air humming softly like a gathering swarm of insects.

I picture another body, beneath another bunched-up white sheet, lying lifeless and abandoned on the dirty gray pavement of Ferguson, Missouri, in the suffocating heat of an early August day.

Michael Brown.

Eighteen years old.

Somebody's son.

Gone.

His body left unattended on the ground for four and a half hours.

I think about his parents—two people I've never met; two people whose appearances I can only vaguely conjure into my mind; a mother, a father. I don't know them, but as a father myself

I know that their hearts have been ravaged, their souls shattered. And I'm certain that one central question knifes through them: How could *they*—meaning the police, meaning us, meaning *me*—leave their son lying in the middle of the street for *four and a half hours*?

By now, they've been given a reason. An explanation. An excuse.

But the question remains.

Crowds—angry, incensed crowds—had gathered near the shooting site, and the people who came to remove the body from the street didn't feel safe. Somebody reported hearing gunshots. The officers at the scene suggested to the people tasked with removing the body that they not leave their vehicle without wearing bulletproof vests. To my knowledge, nobody provided them with bulletproof vests. So they sat in their air-conditioned black sedan, concerned for their own safety, waiting for the police to secure the area so they could do their job.

Any way you try to explain it, Michael Brown's young, black body lay unattended in the street for four and a half hours, beneath that sheet stained with his blood, while the residents of Ferguson gathered to gawk, seethe, anguish, grieve, lash out, scream.

Michael Brown's shooting ignited the fire.

Michael Brown's body burned the city down.

DAY 2

SUNDAY, AUGUST 10, 2014

"THIS IS WAR"

How do we dream ourselves out of this?

JACQUELINE WOODSON
ANOTHER BROOKLYN

THE DAY UNFOLDS like many summer Sundays—slow, calm, restful, reflective, even lazy. Lori and I often go to church on Sunday, but today, feeling worn out after driving back from Milwaukee, I just want to relax, flip through the Sunday papers, catch part of the Cardinals game, stay close to my phone and the news reports, and gear up for work tomorrow morning. Although I don't say anything to Lori, I hope that the people I saw gathering last evening on the streets of Ferguson will not come out again tonight and that the anger and outrage I witnessed has blown over.

Like many of the people I end up speaking to during the day, I want more information, and I want civility to prevail. I want the people who take to the streets to be calm and safe. I want peace. That is, after all, my ultimate role—peacekeeper.

Maybe because I have a premonition or fear the worst, I find myself avoiding the television, even though we keep the news on as ambient noise in the background, with news anchors describing memorials for Michael Brown and a candlelight vigil planned for the evening. As I tinker around the house and putter in the yard, I'm on alert—waiting, I guess, like everyone else, to see what happens next.

Shortly after nightfall, the duty lieutenant calls my cell. I hear the darkness seeping into his voice as he says, "People are back in Ferguson, upset over the shooting. The crowds have gotten bigger. Much bigger. There's looting."

"Okay," I say, massaging the bridge of my nose.

"We've got officers responding," the lieutenant says. "I'm going to respond."

"No," I say, louder than I intended, surprising myself and probably the lieutenant as well. "You live a lot farther away. I'm closer. By the time you get your uniform on and drive all the way to Ferguson, I can be there."

"You sure?"

"Yes."

I look at Lori and see the concern in her eyes, the concern I know every law enforcement officer's spouse feels.

"I'll go."

☆

An hour later I'm standing on West Florissant Avenue, Ferguson's main street, in the eye of a human hurricane. People are running, tripping, falling, flinging themselves at each other, screaming, crying, and cursing against a backdrop of flames that snake up the sides of the convenience store at the QuikTrip gas station, which has been set on fire by some protesters. Fire engulfs the building as the ground throbs and the world erupts.

I gape at the fire: a wall of gold and purple light rising and pulsing, a fountain of flames. The fire crackles and roars, threatening to explode. A burning wind kicks up around it, through it. Although I'm some distance away, the searing golden light stings my eyes.

It feels unreal.

Like a dream.

Police vehicles—too many to count—surround me. Cruisers. Unmarked cars. Tactical vehicles. Police in riot gear and Kevlar vests—their nightsticks holstered, chins jutted, and faces blank behind plastic shields—form a line across the street, defying a massive throng of protesters, some of whom occasionally surge forward. Hundreds of people have converged here—maybe more, perhaps a thousand. I can't tell. I can't focus. I hear store windows smash, and I see looters—many of them shirtless, with red bandannas pulled over the lower half of their faces—running in and out of stores. Some carry cases of beer or soda. Some carry food. But then I see other people who risk arrest simply to provide for their families, or just to *live*. One man carries a package of diapers. Another man, shirtless, his body rope thin, fixes himself a hot dog.

I stand on West Florissant, watching my city burn, and I feel my soul bleed.

Behind me a woman shrieks, "This is war," and then she begins to sob. I turn to look for her, but the line of officers blocks my view.

I turn back to face the crowds and I feel stunned, as if I've been clubbed from behind. The magnitude of the chaos consumes me, causing my legs to quaver. I didn't know what to expect when I arrived here, but it wasn't this. A deep communal hurt has been unearthed, unleashed. A sense of grim destiny thrums through the air. I can't be sure whether I'm hearing the words of every young man in the vicinity or am channeling their thoughts: *Mike Brown could have been me.*

I pivot in another direction now and see several K-9 officers restraining their dogs. The German shepherds growl, snarl, bare their teeth. Suddenly I feel as if I've been transported out of suburban St. Louis 2014 and dropped into the middle of Watts 1965, urban Detroit 1967, or South Central Los Angeles 1992.

The white officers on the scene don't have the same frame of reference and don't realize what police dogs evoke in the hearts of African American citizens.

Shock.

Terror.

Submission.

Standing there with my uniform and badge, I share their feelings. I look at my fellow officers in their riot gear, and I know they're wearing shields to protect themselves, but seeing them now, having abandoned their standard blues for pale-green camouflage, I can't help but view them as soldiers. And to those who live in urban communities, these officers look like occupiers.

Again, they may not realize the message they're sending. They don't see a choice. They are responding by the book, wearing their riot gear for protection against rocks and bottles. Standing in the center of this coiling, deafening chaos, I watch helplessly as the already tenuous link between law enforcement and the community snaps and severs. The police have flooded the neighborhood to guard the gates of the community. But the community itself has been disconnected and set adrift.

For the first time since I was a child, I feel fear.

I have worked SWAT. I have kicked in doors, charged into dark houses, chased armed fugitives into the woods on pitch-black nights, and confronted a cornered perpetrator as he went for his gun, but I have never felt this kind of crippling fear. I've felt the adrenaline pumping and my heart pounding, but I never felt fear.

I'm not afraid for my well-being. I feel a different sort of fear: a deeper fear, an all-encompassing fear. This fear shakes me. Slices me.

I'm afraid we have come to an end—an end to complacency, to good behavior, to the acceptance of an unacceptable status quo, to conditions that are unfair and unequal, conditions that must change. Here on the smoke-filled streets of Ferguson, everything has suddenly and irrevocably changed. The truths I knew—the truths I *thought* I knew, the truths we were told—have been revealed as lies. There is no going back now. The people I see, the people I know, have had enough.

I fear the unknown. Or maybe I fear the known. I can see what happens next. More of this. More fires. More violence. More looting. More chaos. Chaos leads to fear.

Perhaps most of all, I fear that what I see and feel all around me—the people's collective pain—has only just begun, and I don't know what to do for that pain. I feel helpless. I feel lost. I don't know what lies ahead, except more pain. I know we face a troubled tomorrow. I know that for sure. I fear the future—all of our futures.

I fear the future most of all.

★

Later, at a hastily assembled command post in a strip mall across from Target, a short drive from West Florissant, I huddle with the incident commander—Chief Jon Belmar of St. Louis County—and other officers to receive briefings on the rapidly changing situation in Ferguson. Together we search for explanations.

What do we know? Not much. Social media has blown up. Mainstream and national news outlets have descended on Ferguson. So have self-declared news outlets—young people with cell phones and a few thousand Twitter or Facebook followers. People from neighboring towns, feeling outraged or opportunistic or both, have joined the protest. Police officers have rounded up rioters and protesters and made arrests.

I wonder why looters torched the QuikTrip. What does the QuikTrip have to do with Michael Brown? The sad, strange answer is *nothing*. The looters made a mistake. They acted on bad information. They'd heard that Michael Brown stole a pack of cigarillos from the service station. I shake my head. I know that's impossible. I know at QuikTrip they keep all the cigarettes and cigars behind the counter. Michael Brown couldn't get back there. (Later we'll learn that he did steal some cigarillos—from another store. The looters set fire to the wrong store. They burned down the QuikTrip for no reason. Logic does not live in chaos.)

Sometime after 2:00 a.m., with helicopters still hovering over West Florissant and bathing the area in long streams of flood-light, the smell of smoke and ash drifts up from the remains of the QuikTrip, now nothing more than a smoldering shell. The streets are nearly empty; most of the police officers and protesters have scattered. After several hours of offering support, consultation, and observation to the incident commanders, I head for my car. I remain in a state of shock.

Police have made thirty arrests. Two officers were injured by rocks and bottles hurled at them from the shadows. Rioters overturned at least one police car, smashed in the rear windshield of another, and looted and vandalized twelve businesses along West Florissant. The sound of gunfire intermittently cracked through the night.

I pull into my driveway at 2:30, cut the engine, and sit behind the wheel for a few moments. I can't catch my breath. I stare through the windshield into the night, hyperventilating, closing my eyes, trying to calm myself.

"You got to keep moving," I say, murmuring the wisdom of my father, words he lived by, words I live by. "Live moment to moment."

Finally, settling myself, I get out of the car and trudge to the house.

I don't sleep at all.

DAY 3

MONDAY, AUGUST 11, 2014

"THESE PEOPLE"

Empathy must be cultivated.

MICHAEL ERIC DYSON
TEARS WE CANNOT STOP

LYING IN BED, coming out of a fractured daze, I'm not sure if I'm dreaming. Images flicker furiously in front of my eyes—Michael Brown's body lying in the street, protesters clogging West Florissant, rows of police in riot gear, the QuikTrip in flames.

Michael Brown's body lying in the street.

I gasp and rise to a sitting position. The images fade, replaced by the familiarity of my bedroom. I feel numb. And then a thick sense of doom grips me.

Life as I know it has changed.

Today I will not report to my usual job as a troop commander in the Missouri State Highway Patrol, overseeing more than three hundred employees dedicated to the primary mission of promoting highway safety. Instead I will report to Ferguson, to Chief Jon Belmar, the incident commander.

Incident commander.

The word feels flimsy, inadequate.

I blink myself into reality.

Reality.

I'm not sure what that means anymore.

As I lower my feet to the floor and rise, allowing my legs to carry me toward the bathroom, a heaviness descends. Something enormous weighs me down, a gravity I cannot grasp.

At the command post, I'm assigned to provide administrative support for Chief Belmar. One of my first responsibilities is to designate and deploy groups of troopers and one of our SWAT teams to Ferguson. From this point forward, I will coordinate whatever trooper presence Chief Belmar requests and keep my command staff informed of new developments. When not on the phone, I will attend briefings with representatives from the two other main agencies who have been assigned here—St. Louis City and St. Louis County.

Jon Belmar maintains a calm and steady presence, even though he's operating in a well of tension, uncertainty, and—at times—chaos. The sheer number of people on the scene threatens to overload our circuits. In addition to an ever-changing array of protesters, citizens, and media gathered outside, representatives from more than fifty law enforcement agencies have arrived in Ferguson, many of them self-deployed officers who have come to offer their help.

The morning ticks by. We discuss preparations—what we might do *if* and *when*. We consider various contingencies, with everyone from our assembled group of experienced law-enforcement leaders offering suggestions, tactics, and potential responses for both best-case possibilities and worst-case scenarios.

Nothing feels familiar or even exactly appropriate. I sense that Jon, like the rest of us, is struggling to find his footing. No one here has ever faced anything remotely like what we saw last night. We are in uncharted territory.

Somebody refers to the National Incident Management System (NIMS), a set of procedures put out by the Federal Emergency Management Agency (FEMA). We have adhered to the first step of the NIMS guidelines—setting up a command post—but last night's protests seem to take us beyond the parameters of the NIMS protocol. During a break from the briefings, I wander through the small command post, feeling on edge, antsy, and far away from what is happening outside.

Too far away.

☆

In the afternoon, I drive up West Florissant and pull over to what had been the QuikTrip gas station less than twenty-four hours ago. I want to see what remains in the light of day. I squint into the sun and see a charred husk of a building. A few people mill around the still-smoking structure, taking pictures with their phones.

Across the street, several business owners sweep up glass and debris outside their shattered front windows and splintered doors. Some nail plywood sheets over the openings. Others walk through their stores and back out to the sidewalk, shaking their heads in disbelief, their shoes crunching through the shards of glass. I hear a smattering of voices. They talk about the damage, the looters, the night. They look shell shocked. To me, West Florissant looks like a bombed-out street in Iraq or Syria.

I look back at the QuikTrip, and a moment of disbelief swamps me.

Has this really happened?

I picture myself filling up my car at those gas pumps or buying gum or Life Savers at the counter inside, strolling down the street, stepping into a store to buy a soda.

I suddenly feel violated. The pain I felt oozing from others on the street last night is my pain. The protests, the *unrest*, are happening to me—in my heart and in my home. I wear the uniform and the badge, and I'm sworn to protect and serve and keep the peace. But Ferguson is not some isolated, foreign dot on a map. It's my hometown. My place. Ferguson belongs to me. It lives within me.

All day long I hear the undercurrent of a distant, approaching drumbeat.

Footsteps.

More and more footsteps.

As each hour passes, more people arrive—first the protesters and then the police, the press, and the politicians. Some have come because they believe they must be here—including a state senator, whose presence surprises me. Others I believe have come only to be seen. Three days after Michael Brown's death, Ferguson has become a kind of landing point.

We have chosen to wage the war here.

Nobody says those words out loud, but nobody has to—it's what I feel, what everyone feels. The nation has chosen Ferguson as a battleground. The name alone has become an instant symbol, a statement.

More people arrive by the minute, by the carload, by the busload, and West Florissant teems with protesters. As night falls, the anger and pain simmer, boil, and then explode, like a lid flying off of an untended pressure cooker. The heat of the summer day scorching the pavement equals the heat of the anger pulsing through the mass of people who now begin to advance. That surging anger—that pain—has become their engine.

A day later, still no new information about the shooter has surfaced. The community narrative remains unrefuted: *A young, unarmed black man was murdered by the police.*

That cannot happen here. But it has.

⭐

By late afternoon, the fury returns. Protesters begin to chant, "Whose streets? *Our* streets!"

Rioters mix with peaceful protesters, and soon the police can't tell the difference. Rioters heave bottles. They sling rocks. They fire guns in the air. Shirts off, fists waving, voices raised, the people advance in waves with signs held high, chanting, "Hands up, don't shoot!"

The police on the streets in their camouflage riot gear form a human barricade. They brace themselves behind their shields, like soldiers preparing for battle. I know what's running through their minds, but they don't know what to say. They don't have the right words, the right sentiments, the right experience to draw from. They want to voice the confusion they feel as they try to do what they see as their responsibility.

We didn't burn the QuikTrip.

We didn't loot the stores.

We're here to restore order.

I see both sides. I belong to both sides. But there shouldn't *be* sides. Taking sides implies a winner and a loser. There are no winners here. Even if some police see it as a battle to be won, I see only a no-win situation.

I feel as if I'm floundering, trying to figure this out. There are no by-the-book rules to guide us. NIMS doesn't seem to be enough. Or even right. Nobody has written a manual for Ferguson.

★

Before the officers lob tear gas into the crowd that gathers near the QuikTrip, and before they shoot PepperBalls and beanbag rounds into a mob on West Florissant, I drift in and out of pockets of people. Referring to Michael Brown's shooting, young men shout, "We want answers!" But other young men, seeing me, approach and don't talk about Michael Brown at all. They talk about their lives. One says, "You don't understand. We don't have *jobs*!"

At first, their pleas knock me back. "I do understand," I say after a moment. "I'm listening."

"No, man, you can't understand. You *have* a job."

"Talk to me. Tell me."

Before our conversation can continue, these young men are swallowed up by the crowd, or they see the police advancing and run. Another young man, who looks to be in his early twenties, about the same age as my son, comes right up to me, stares at me for a moment, and then says, "Sir."

"Yes?"

"For the first time in my life, I feel that I'm part of something."

I find his words heartbreaking.

Before I can respond, I feel someone's hand on my shoulder.

"We have to go."

I turn and face a trooper I know well, a man I have served

with for twenty-seven years. A white man. He and his wife and Lori and I have often attended work functions together. We've laughed and enjoyed each other's company. I consider him a friend.

"What?" I say, not understanding.

"We have to *go*."

"Why?"

I catch a whiff of it then. His fear. Oozing out and engulfing us both. Nearby, more people amass, spilling onto the street. I sense people moving in behind us. Troopers.

"You're comfortable here with these people," he says. "A lot of us are not."

These people.

I can't speak. I feel as if he has slapped me across the face. I start to say something but hold myself back. The trooper outranks me. We need to talk. But we cannot have that talk right now, in the middle of all this chaos. The trooper pivots away toward two other officers. I see a third trooper, another white man, who shifts his weight uncomfortably. I can tell he has heard our conversation because he looks away, his eyes fixed on the pavement.

"You okay?" I ask him.

He says nothing. He keeps his head down.

The first trooper rushes toward me again. "I told you we have to leave."

At this moment, I know that everything in my life has changed. This man, my coworker, a man I've called a friend for twenty-seven years, no longer sees *me*. He sees through my uniform. He sees only the color of my skin.

I can no longer help myself. Heart racing, I say, "What do you mean by *these people*?"

"I'm saying that the people here are not going to accept me the way they accept you."

"*These people*," I say again softly.

"You're being overly—" He tilts his head and glares at me. "Are you calling me a bigot? Do you think I'm a bigot?"

I don't want to answer him. I don't want to continue this conversation. I want to flee. I turn away before I say something I will regret, but I know I've already lost a friend. Then I realize: *He has never truly been a friend.*

We drive back to the command post in silence. As we ride, a scene from my childhood flashes before me: I am in grade school. My family has moved from an all-black neighborhood in St. Louis City to an all-white neighborhood in the suburbs. We are, in fact, the only black family on our street, and my brother, sister, and I are the only black kids in our new school. My first week in third grade, one of the kids calls me the N-word. I've heard the word before, of course, but only from other black kids who said it in a familiar, almost joking way. I have never heard the word directed at me with hatred.

That's how I feel driving back to command with that trooper. He hadn't used the word, but he might as well have.

We pull up in front of the command post, and I storm out of the car. I hurry into the storefront that serves as our on-site headquarters and find my boss talking on the telephone. I mouth that I need to speak to him, and I pace the room, fidgety, on edge, as I wait for him to complete his call. I rub my hand over my shaved head, and it comes up slick. Even with the air-conditioning on full blast I can feel myself sweating. The trooper steps inside the door and walks over to me.

"You didn't answer my question," he says. "I want to know. Do you think I'm a bigot?"

I feel my face burn. "When you say *these people*," I reply as evenly as I can, "you're answering the question yourself."

He starts to speak, but I cut him off. "You may not even be conscious of what you said, or the words you used, but certain words have certain meanings. The meaning here was clear."

He looks at me hard. He says nothing, but his eyes narrow, his pupils becoming like pinpricks.

"Emotions are high right now," I say. "People are upset. There's a lot of anger. But there is no way we should have left that street."

"I felt uncomfortable—"

"With *these people*—"

"YES."

Speaking barely above a whisper, my voice cracking, I say, "So, if I didn't have my uniform on, if you didn't know me—"

I don't want to continue. I want to end this conversation. I want to get away from him. Instead, I lean in and continue.

"I was talking to some young men out there. We *need* to talk to them. We need to hear them out. We can't run away from them."

He stares at me and I stare back. And then my entire body sags. I feel as if my world has tipped over.

My thoughts jumbled, my anger swelling, I spin and head toward the bathroom—passing my boss, who has finished his phone call and has been listening to us. I shove my shoulder into the bathroom door, duck inside, and lock the door.

I pace a few steps, drop into a crouch, and start to cry.

I lower my head into my chest and weep.

I weep over the loss of a friend.

I weep for a world that no longer exists.

I weep because I feel completely and brutally alone.

And then I mutter a prayer.

Please, Lord. Help me.

These are the only words I can find.

★

I dab a wet paper towel over my eyes as I study myself in the mirror. I look ravaged. My eyes are filmy and bloodshot. I sigh, crumple the paper towel, toss it into the trash, and walk out of the bathroom. My boss is waiting outside the door.

"I overheard the two of you," he says.

"I know," I say. "I'm sorry."

"No, I'm sorry."

"I just . . . I didn't like how he kept saying *these people*."

My boss nods, and I can see that his eyes are bloodshot too.

"Ron," he says, "this is just starting. A lot of people are afraid."

We look at each other, and then the two of us, my boss and I, two seasoned highway patrol troopers, a black man and a white man, grab each other and hug.

And then we both begin to cry.

DAY 4

TUESDAY, AUGUST 12, 2014

"WHY AM I DIFFERENT?"

I want to look happily forward. I want to be optimistic. I want to have a dream.

EDWIDGE DANTICAT
"MESSAGE TO MY DAUGHTERS"

MONDAY ENDS WITH MORE ARRESTS, looting, chaos, and pain. I get home after midnight, still shaken by my encounter with the trooper—a friend, I thought, but in reality, a man I never knew. I climb into bed, my mind racing, fearing for tomorrow, seeing no conclusion, no good outcome, no answers. Tossing fitfully, trying not to wake Lori, I look up at the ceiling . . . and something comes over me, a kind of presence, dropping gently onto me like a mist. I shade my eyes with my hand and say, very softly, "Sometimes, Lord, I get busy and I forget to pray. That has been happening to me. It's been happening for a while. Maybe it's always happened."

I feel a tear trickle down my cheek. I blot it with my thumb and say, "I have no words right now. I feel lost. All I see are dead ends and darkness. I don't know where I'm going. I don't even know if I'm facing the right direction. But starting tomorrow I am going to get down on my knees every day. That I promise."

I close my eyes and sigh.

Something my dad used to say echoes in my mind: *Keep on moving forward.*

I will, Dad.

But before I can do that, I need to go back.

★

When I was seven years old, I lived with my parents, Roscoe and Annie; my brother, Bernard; and my sister, Regina, in St. Louis, in one half of a long, narrow, railroad-style house, with the living room in the front as you walked in and the kitchen in the back, facing a small yard and an alley. I shared a room in the basement with Bernard, two years younger, while Regina, two years older, rated a bedroom to herself upstairs near the kitchen.

Money mattered. My parents struggled, but I wouldn't say we were poor. Even when my parents both got laid off, they still managed to put food on the table. For a time, we relied on food stamps and took the free cheese and snacks that volunteers gave out at church. And sometimes my parents had to make difficult choices.

I remember one especially cold night during the winter, we went to a little burger restaurant called the Red Barn. After we finished our burgers and fries, we all just sat at our table. My parents seemed in no hurry to leave.

Finally, bored, I asked, "Can we go?"

"Not yet," my father said.

We stayed until closing time, when one of the restaurant workers wheeled out a bucket and mop and started swabbing down the floor.

When we got home and opened the front door, I remember a chill rolling over me like a frosty wave. In the winter, my parents sometimes had to choose between food and heat. That month, they chose food. Shivering, my brother, sister, and I huddled together in one bed, wearing sweaters, tightening the covers around us, summoning our combined body heat to keep warm.

As the middle child, I assumed the role of referee when my brother and sister went at it. Regina at nine—older, worldly, and sophisticated—had little tolerance for five-year-old Bernard, a fiery handful with a nonstop motor and a nose for trouble. I didn't mind playing peacemaker because I modeled myself after my father, who had become a campus police officer at St. Louis University. I looked up to him. (That's not accurate: I wanted to *be* him.) Whenever we played "Family," my favorite game, I assumed the role of Dad, slipping my small feet into my father's shoes and clopping authoritatively around the house.

Outside the family, people saw me as quiet. I suppose I was, but I also had a keen, observant eye. Even if I didn't say much, I took in everything. People called me "the good kid," and I tried to live up to the title. I *was* a good kid—most of the time.

One day, my mother announced that Regina, Bernard, and I would be going to the circus with our church group. We had no money for food or snacks once we got there, so my mother fed us before we left.

As we headed out the door, I passed my parents' bedroom and spotted a twenty-dollar bill on the dresser. I paused, looked around, darted into their room, snatched the twenty, and stuffed it into my pocket. At the circus, I waited for the right moment and revealed to my sister and brother that I had found a twenty-dollar bill on the ground. I was an instant hero. I used the money to treat myself, Bernard, and Regina to ice cream and candy, coming home with only a couple of dollars in change.

The moment we walked into the house, we could hear our mother sobbing. We found her and our father in their bedroom. Through her tears, my mother said that she had left twenty dollars on the dresser and now it was gone. She blamed herself, saying she must have misplaced it.

"That was the last twenty dollars we had," she said. "I don't know what we're going to do."

Then my sister, in total innocence, blurted out that I had found twenty dollars at the circus.

Of course my parents knew immediately what had happened.

"Where did you get that money?" my father asked.

"I found it."

"I'm going to ask you one more time," my father said, his voice level. "Where did you get the money?"

I answered by bursting into tears. I knew I had been doing something wrong when I stuffed the twenty into my pocket. But only as I saw my mother sobbing did I realize that I had actually *stolen* the money. I felt like a thief.

At a minimum, I expected a severe whupping at the hand of my father, the dispenser of punishments. But he didn't lift a finger. He knew in this case that any punishment would pale in comparison to the pain I felt seeing my mother cry.

A few days later, after the pain had subsided into a crippling sense of guilt, I was surprised to discover that my parents didn't hold anything against me. In fact, our relationship hadn't changed at all. They had expressed their disappointment, but then they had given me a second chance. I was afraid they would snub me, ignore me, or speak to me only in anger; but they treated me as they always had—with love and kindness.

I learned a powerful lesson that day: I am their son. They loved me and believed in me, and they accepted that people make mistakes.

How often in our culture do we condemn young people after they make a mistake? How often do we give young people—especially young people of color—a second chance? Society often defines people by their mistakes. Sadly, I've seen that mistakes can determine the entire course of a person's life.

My parents not only gave me a second chance but would also soon give me a *third* chance.

★

A year or so later, when I was about eight, our family's financial situation had improved enough that my parents enrolled my brother, sister, and me at a private Catholic school. I don't remember much about my time there, except I felt like an outcast among my neighborhood friends because I went to a different school than they did, and they gave me grief about it. At the Catholic school, probably because I really didn't want to be there, I acted out.

One day, my second-grade teacher asked me to do something—or stop doing something—and I refused. She reached for my arm. I defiantly swung my hand away and accidentally slapped her wrist, smashing the crystal on her watch. Upset, she sent me to the principal, who called my mother—and not for the first time.

When my father got home that night, he walked into my room and handed me a brown paper shopping bag.

"Put all your things into this bag," he said.

"Why?"

"Because you're moving out. You're not going to be living here anymore."

Then he left me alone in my room.

Stunned, I slowly started filling up the bag. I put in a few clothes, a favorite toy, my toothbrush, and then, clutching the bag to my chest, I walked slowly into the living room where my parents and siblings sat waiting.

"Say good-bye to your brother and sister," my father said.

I looked up at him but didn't move. He tilted his head toward Bernard and Regina.

I walked over to them and whispered good-bye. They both immediately started crying. I lost it. I threw my arms around my brother and then hugged my sister.

"Say good-bye to your mother," my father said.

I went over to her and stood in front of her—speechless. She bit her lip and then began to sob.

Tears gushed down my cheeks, and I began to wail.

"Where . . . where am I . . ."

I couldn't finish the sentence.

"Let's go," my father said, pulling me away from my mother. He guided me out to the driveway, and we got into the car.

As we drove away from the house, with my paper shopping bag on my lap, I managed to gain control of myself. My father drove slowly and said nothing. He stared ahead, his gaze grim and determined. After a while, he turned a corner and parked in front of a large, imposing building.

"We're here," my father said.

I hunched down and squinted through the window, trying to make out the lettering on the building.

"This is the police station," my father said. "You're going to jail."

The tears came again, this time in sheets. I heard my father climb out of the car and close his door. Within seconds, the passenger door opened, and he ushered me out of the car, leading me by the arm into the police station and up to the front desk where the officer on duty looked up from some paperwork he was doing. He nodded as if he were expecting us.

"Is this him?"

"Yes," my father said.

"Okay then," the officer said. "I'll take it from here."

"Good luck, Son," my father said. He offered his hand and I shook it. Then he turned and walked out of the police station.

I let out a wail, my entire body shaking with sobs. I wanted to run and catch up to my father, but before I could move, the officer came out from behind his desk, took my arm, and steered me across the room. I tried to walk, but my legs felt as heavy as lead.

"Hurry up," the officer said.

I gasped and one last cry gushed forth before I could contain myself. My chest heaving, I allowed the police officer to escort me down a corridor toward a jail cell. I managed to catch my breath and swiped at my tears. I felt broken, destroyed—like an actual criminal.

This is for real, I said to myself. *This is happening. My life is over.*

We stopped in front of the cell. The officer pulled out a ring of keys and inserted one into the lock. He jiggled the lock; I heard a click, and the cell door swung open, creaking and clanging. The officer stepped aside and nodded—first at me and then at the inside of the cell.

I looked into the cell and saw a slab connected to the wall

(which I assumed was the bed), a filthy washbasin, and a grubby toilet with no seat. An icy chill streaked down the length of my spine, as if someone had dropped an ice cube inside my shirt.

"Get in there," the officer said.

I hesitated and my stomach lurched. I thought I was about to be sick. The officer put his hand on my shoulder.

"This isn't where you want to be, is it?" he said.

"No, sir," I mumbled.

"Then you need to start making better decisions. And you need to listen to your parents."

"Yes, sir."

"Let's go," the officer said.

He closed the door to the cell with a crash that startled me. Then he led me back to his desk, and my father was waiting there. I threw myself at my dad, gripping his legs with every ounce of strength I could find.

When we got home, I ran into the living room, where I found my mother, brother, and sister still sitting in the same places—and still crying.

I can't say I became a perfect child after that, but I made sure that I never stepped far enough over the line to get me anywhere close to that jail again.

★

Right before Christmas when I was nine, my parents bought a house on a corner lot in a predominantly white suburb of St. Louis. We were the only black family on our street. We moved for the larger space, bigger yard, better schools, and safer streets. In other words, my parents moved for us kids, for our future.

We moved in the middle of the school year and would start at our new school in January. But first my parents decided to celebrate this new start—this new life—by taking a Christmas trip to visit my mom's family in San Francisco. As we boarded the train in St. Louis, I tried to grab hold of all the *newness* swirling around me—new home, new neighborhood, new school, new friends. I was taking a cross-country train ride for the first time, visiting a city I'd never seen and relatives I'd never met.

Christmas in California.

A trip I will never forget.

Our relatives met us with two cars outside the train station in San Francisco. My mom got into the first car with her sisters, while my brother, sister, and I scrunched into the backseat of the second car with my cousin. My dad settled into the front seat next to my uncle, who was driving. I remember the car pulling away from the curb and into the flow of San Francisco traffic, but after that, my memory is a blur. Scattered images and sounds topple over each other, flashing before my eyes, blinding me.

The car lurching.

The jolt of impact.

The deafening crash.

The crunch of metal.

Screams.

Our bodies springing forward.

Sirens.

Hands clawing at us, pulling us out from the mashed-in backseat.

I can see my brother, my sister, and my cousin standing outside on the street, with my uncle's car listing at an ungodly angle in front of us, impaled on a guardrail. The front end crushed. Glass everywhere.

Where's Dad?

I envision my mother in the other car with her sisters, laughing, driving home, blissfully unaware.

More sirens wailing.

Yellow police tape flapping, closing us in.

Fire trucks roaring, surrounding us. A scramble of firefighters everywhere.

Police cruisers screeching, lined up in rows.

A crowd.

Hands grappling at the front doors of the dismembered car. A fireman approaching with a crowbar. Another with an ax.

Where is Dad?

My uncle and my father trapped in the front seat.

I see no movement.

Then I see my uncle's head bobbing. But I don't see . . .

Where's . . . DAD!

My disembodied voice.

Howling.

We spent Christmas Day at the hospital, my father hooked up to tubes and machines that gurgled and beeped. The moment I saw him, I began to cry. My father, who was *my world*, had shrunk to something small and frail. He extended his hand toward me.

"I'm all right, Son," he said. "I'm going to be all right."

I ran to him. He gripped my hand, smothering my fingers. I wanted to be strong. I didn't want to cry. But I couldn't stop myself.

Finally, breathing hard, my sobbing now intermittent,

I dragged a chair to my dad's bedside. Neither one of us could say very much. I stayed with him for what seemed like hours, until he got tired. Then the nurse and my mother said we should leave so my dad could sleep.

In the hallway, I asked my mom, "Is he really going to be all right?"

My mother paused . . . too long.

"Yes," she said.

At some point later, she told me the truth. My father couldn't walk. He had been paralyzed, and the doctors didn't know whether he would ever walk again. They sounded optimistic, though, she said, and the lead doctor predicted that my dad would walk again, especially given his powerful determination and the fact that he was only thirty-five years old.

I know he'll walk again, I told myself. *I know it. Dad's a fighter. He* will *walk again.*

But the doctors couldn't promise anything. All they could say was that my dad would have to stay in the hospital for several more weeks. We extended our time in San Francisco through the end of the year, but then we had to return to our new house, our new neighborhood, our new school—our new *life*—while Dad stayed in California in his hospital bed.

Meanwhile, my uncle, who had caused all this, had been released from the hospital with minor injuries—able to walk, free to return to his family and his life.

As a child, taking it all in, I struggled to comprehend how our family structure had been so suddenly disrupted and disordered. My father's career as a police officer had been put on hold, his future uncertain. All of our futures were now uncertain. Who *was* my father now? What kind of a man would he be? I had lost the father I knew.

For the first time in my life, I felt hatred. I hated my uncle—this man I had never met, who had mutilated my father's legs, ruined his life and his family.

And now I had to return to St. Louis—to everything new and uncertain—without a father.

★

When we got home from San Francisco, we found our sidewalk and driveway buried under snow. At first, I didn't register what that meant. Any other time, my dad would have put on his parka, slung the snow shovel over his shoulder, headed outside, and cleared the snow away in rhythmic, machinelike movements.

No more.

My mother and I trudged outside together, crunching down the driveway through snow that came halfway up my boots. Mom jabbed the blade of the shovel into the packed-in snow, jiggled the blade, hauled up a small mountain of snow, grunted softly, and tossed the snow onto the lawn.

Then she handed the snow shovel to me.

I fumbled with the handle, copied her technique, and lifted a tiny lump of snow, which I dumped to the side.

Mom nodded. "Keep at it," she said. "This is your job now."

I wanted to protest, but I had no choice. My sister would be doing double duty in the kitchen, helping Mom prepare meals and cleaning the house. Seven-year-old Bernard would help me, but not really. The burden of keeping our sidewalk and driveway clear and usable in winter fell squarely on me.

I thought of my favorite game—"Family"—in which I always

played the dad. I exhaled, sliced the shovel into a clump of snow on the driveway, dug out a more substantial hill of snow, and flung it onto Mom's pile. I was no longer playing a game. This was real.

☆

The first time I walked into my new school, time slowed. The school day seemed to last a week. Everywhere I walked, I felt eyes on me—people staring, assessing, judging. Hating. I felt their hatred drilling into me.

I didn't know where to look. Sometimes I looked at the floor. Sometimes I looked straight ahead, past the blank faces that flooded my vision. Maybe someone said hello; maybe someone smiled. I don't know. I didn't hear or see that. I heard only the hatred—and the word. It was part of our vocabulary back in our old neighborhood, used in fun with my black friends. The younger kids used the word because the older kids incorporated it into their everyday speech without a second thought, a substitute for *man*. They used the word lightly, as a punch line, as a verbal tic, but never ever hatefully. Here at my new school, the white kids spewed the word at me like poison. The word burned. The word singed my heart.

I walked straight ahead. I couldn't let anyone see my fear. But fear was all I felt. It filled me up and threatened to spill out. The fear made my lip tremble. I bit my lip until it bled.

When I got home, my mother asked me about my first day.

"Why did I leave my old school?" I said.

☆

The first time I experienced hatred directed toward me, it was from other nine-year-olds, who hated me for no reason other than the color of my skin. They spit *the word* at me because I didn't look like them.

But children don't come into this world knowing how to hate.

Somebody has to teach them.

☆

The days dragged by. Other vile words raked me, wounded me, sickened me. Some I hadn't heard before, but I knew what they meant. At school, I lived in constant fear. And then I started to feel something else. Something worse. I started to feel alone.

At night, safe at home, I asked my mother to stop the hatred. I asked her to fix it. She started to cry.

"I can't," she said. "I don't know how."

She hugged me, and we held on to each other for a long time. Clinging to her, I wondered whether my father would be able to fix it.

During the second week at our new school, my mother baked a chocolate cake for my sister to take to her class because it was her turn to provide a snack. After school, Regina came home with the whole cake, uncut.

"Nobody would touch it," she said.

I knew why but didn't say anything.

"They wouldn't touch the cake because I'm *black*," my sister said, pressing down on the word, making sure my mother and I heard and felt her pain and her fury.

"What about the teacher?" my mother asked.

"Especially the teacher," my sister said.

☆

One day as I shoveled our sidewalk, snow flurries pecking my face, a police car drove slowly past our house and pulled into a driveway at the far corner of our block. I leaned on the shovel as the driver's door opened and a state trooper stepped out of the car. He closed his car door and saw me watching him. He grinned and waved. I waved back. He turned and went into his house. I liked the way he strode up his driveway, his back straight and strong. He looked regal. He looked like a soldier. A warrior.

From then on, whenever I saw the trooper who lived on our street, I made sure to wave, and he always waved back.

☆

Two months after the accident, my father came home in a wheelchair.

When I saw him, I didn't cry, but my stomach flipped. He looked diminished. I thought about how we used to spend our time together. Everything involved physical activity—tossing a football, playing catch, shooting hoops, puttering around the house, shoveling snow, mowing the lawn, pulling weeds.

You can be my legs.

I don't know whether my father said those words or I imagined him saying them. But I didn't want to be his legs. I wanted him to have his own powerful legs. His old legs.

I wished I could have invented a time machine. I would only ask to go back in time three months, that's all. I wouldn't get on that train for San Francisco. I wouldn't spend Christmas in California. I wouldn't move into the house in the suburbs. That's all I wanted—to go back in time three months.

Instead, I witnessed a miracle. In no time at all, my father abandoned the wheelchair, stood to his feet, and *walked*, leaning and supporting himself with both arms on a metal contraption he used to traverse the living room, the kitchen, the whole house.

Shortly after that, he graduated from the walker to two canes, and finally to one cane. He walked slowly, deliberately, his steps strong and determined. He still couldn't run or play sports, but he could walk. My father was a miracle.

★

People drove their cars through our front yard. Teenagers, mostly. They tore up our lawn, leaving muddy tire tracks that looked like scars. The cars would gash our grass, digging gullies and sink-holes, and run over anything we planted. These teenagers would roll down their windows as they tore across our yard, scream the word at our door, and then drive off laughing.

My brother, sister, and I would cower in the kitchen. We felt vulnerable, exposed, attacked. My mother and father said nothing, but I could see the fear, anger, and confusion on their faces. I wanted to ask, *Why are they doing this?* but by then I knew that nobody had the answer.

One afternoon several months after we moved in, Bernard, Regina, and I were playing in the basement while Mom prepared dinner in the kitchen. Suddenly I heard a thud and a crack from outside, followed by a gurgle and a whoosh. Someone shouted a muffled curse, and I heard my mother yell something to my father. Regina, Bernard, and I scrambled upstairs to find Mom fiddling with the kitchen faucet.

"The water's been cut off," she said.

My father limped into the room, stopped, and stared out the window. I followed his eyes.

Several people were milling around outside on our lawn. Within seconds, more people arrived, and then even more, until a mob filled the yard. Sirens screeched; red and blue lights flickered through our windows and across our faces. Police officers began to filter in among the people on our lawn.

I could see now that a car had rammed into the fire hydrant on our corner and knocked it over. Water gushed from the top of the decapitated hydrant. I looked at the crowd amassed on our lawn. Every person I could see was white. Nobody came to our door. Nobody offered to help. Nobody took responsibility for leveling the fire hydrant and ripping up our lawn.

"We have no water," my mother said, her voice shaking. "All these people—"

"Everybody stay in the house," my father said.

My mother blinked at him. "What are you going to do?"

"Just stay here," he said. "And keep away from the windows," he added, almost as an afterthought.

"They could've hit our home," my mother said softly, her voice quaking.

My father retrieved his cane, which was leaning against the kitchen table, tapped the bottom on the floor as if for luck, then went to the front door, opened it, and stepped outside.

I started to follow him, but my mother pulled me back gently. After a moment, I wriggled away and stretched as tall as I could to look out the window.

"Nobody said anything," my mother muttered. "Why didn't they tell us? Why didn't somebody knock on the door and tell us?"

Outside, my father limped forward and stepped into the crowd. He walked slowly, calmly, with great purpose. The crowd parted, allowing him to approach a police officer. My father seemed so alone—so isolated; but at that moment, he also seemed regal.

More than forty years later, I still remember my father's solitary walk into the middle of that crowd of people on our lawn—many of them hostile, some calling him the word. I see his walk as an act of courage and of faith.

His walk will always inspire me and guide me. His walk will give me direction and resolve. His walk will give me courage and faith.

In the aftermath of Michael Brown's death, I can see my life coming full circle. I see my father beginning the circle, walking without fear into the mob amassed on our lawn. I see myself completing the circle, walking without fear down the streets of Ferguson. I never could have made that walk if I hadn't seen my father's walk first.

That night in my childhood home, after the crowd had dispersed, I sat in the living room with my family. Earlier, the police had told my father that they'd apprehended the kid who drove into the fire hydrant. Nobody knew whether he would be punished—and we never found out. We never heard from him. He never apologized, nor did he or anyone else offer to pay for the damage to our yard. No one showed any concern or uttered of sympathy. No one offered to help us in any way. But I did hear several people call us names, including the word, as they left our yard.

"Why are we different?" I asked my parents that night, and I saw them struggle to answer.

"I *look* different," I said, "but I do the same things as everybody else. I eat the same foods as everybody else. I play the same games, the same sports. I watch TV like everybody else. I live in a house like everybody else's. I hurt the same, I feel the same, I pray to the same God. I say the Lord's Prayer before I go to bed, the same as every other kid I know. So—"

I swallowed, then choked on the words. *Why am I different?*

★

On Tuesday, August 12, the fourth day of the protests in Ferguson, organizers lead hundreds of people to Clayton, the county seat, demanding criminal prosecution for the officer who shot Michael Brown. As of now, the Ferguson police have not released the officer's name. The protesters carry signs and hold their hands in the air, shouting, "Hands up, don't shoot!" referring to reports that Michael Brown had his hands in the air when the officer shot him.

After a spokesperson informs the crowd that Tom Jackson, the Ferguson police chief, will reveal the name of the officer shortly, the protesters march peacefully and without incident. The spokesperson returns later and announces that the officer's name will not be released until the following day. The protesters object, insist, shout, and demand answers, their frustration and anger as palpable and real as the heat that simmers up from the sidewalk; but they remain peaceful.

Around noon, the Reverend Al Sharpton meets with Michael Brown's parents in Ferguson. He holds a news conference and asks for calm and for people to end the rioting. Referring to Michael Brown, he says, "Some of us are making the story 'how mad we are' rather than how promising he was."

Later in the day, President Obama issues a statement, pleading for calm, urging people to "remember this young man through reflection and understanding."

For the most part, I stay at the command post. When I do go outside during daylight hours, I see pockets of protesters—including young mothers pushing their babies in strollers. Young children under the age of ten trail them, holding signs that say

"Don't shoot!" I see clusters of young men running with their shirts off, sweat beading on their chests in the stifling afternoon heat, their fists raised, their movements jerky and anxious.

For the briefest moment, the civility of the protests in Clayton, the appearance of Rev. Sharpton, the young moms with their children, and the exuberant but peaceful young men on the streets lull me into thinking that tonight will be different, that we will see an evening of calm and peaceful protests. But when night falls, this disparate group of people with their melting pot of issues boils into rage and ugliness, and everything turns dark.

The crowd grows until West Florissant teems with people. Tonight the crowd appears to be the largest, the most impatient, the most violent.

The police presence has grown as well, with rows of police forming from city, state, and county agencies. Lines of officers in riot gear and camouflage assemble, with armored vehicles grinding behind them, canine patrol officers alongside them, and SWAT sharpshooters perched atop police vehicles.

Some of the rioters, hopped up on adrenaline and anger and furious at the militarized police presence, converge and charge the lines of law enforcement, hurling bottles and Molotov cocktails. The homemade explosives shatter on the ground—popping, spurting flames, and sending up clouds of smoke. A few bottles hit officers directly or carom off their riot shields. Through it all, the ground rumbles in a deep, vibrating bass, a hip-hop beat, as hundreds of people start running—some seemingly going in circles, others still coming at the line of officers who block their way and attempt to stifle their fury.

The police, starting with the SWAT teams, respond in the moment. Through bullhorns, police commanders tell the

protesters to disperse—*now, immediately*—but either the protesters refuse to move or they don't retreat fast enough, because
suddenly the police fire a barrage of tiny nonlethal projectiles
that screech through the air and rain down on the crowd. Tear
gas canisters follow, whistling through the night. Smoky, noxious
clouds rise, engulfing the street—the protesters coughing, choking, stumbling, vomiting. The scene is something out of a fever
dream.

As I take it all in—the chaos, the panic, the despair, the fear,
the pain—a deep sorrow grips me. Somehow I know this is only
the beginning. In my heart, I know what's coming.

It's as if I'm looking out a window and seeing in the distance
a dark, massive, malevolent cloud moving slowly . . . slowly . . .
but starting to pick up speed.

I see the storm of storms coming.

I see it, but I can't stop it.

Back at the command post, Major Bret Johnson—my boss and
my friend—notices the troubled look in my eye.

"What, Ron?" he asks.

I want to say, *There's a hellacious storm coming. It's going to be
bad, so very bad—we can't imagine how bad. I just hope we can all
endure it.*

"I can't—" I stop, swallow. "I can't explain it."

I get home late, after 2:00 a.m. I don't want to wake Lori, so I
go into another room. To be honest, I don't want her to see my
concern, my fear. I close the door and drop to my knees. I close
my eyes.

I have no idea what to say.

I have no idea what to pray.

For some time now, I have questioned my faith. I have

questioned God. Not his existence, but his intentions. I have felt . . . doubt.

And I have wondered why.

Why was my dad hurt so badly in that accident?

When I asked my mom that question as a child, she told me, "Things happen for a reason."

On my knees, I hear my mom's voice: "God will never leave you alone."

I have never gone this deep into my faith before. I feel myself drawing closer to God, closer than I have ever felt.

"Please, Lord," I say finally. "Please—"

I go blank.

I take a deep breath, exhale, and the words rush out in a whisper: "Please help all of us endure the storm that I know is coming."

I pause.

"And Dad . . . and Bernard . . . please . . . watch over me. Guide me. I need your strength."

DAY 5

WEDNESDAY, AUGUST 13, 2014

WAITING FOR THE STORM

*The ultimate measure of a man is not where he
stands in moments of comfort and convenience
but where he stands at times of challenge
and controversy.*

MARTIN LUTHER KING, JR.
STRENGTH TO LOVE

LATE IN THE MORNING, as I drive to work, my cell phone
rings. I glance at my dashboard readout and see my father-in-
law's name and number. I click on the Bluetooth.

"Hey, Pops."

"How you doing?"

"Okaaaay." The word comes out in three syllables, an
involuntary sigh.

"I've been thinking," my father-in-law says.

Lori's dad, a retired police officer, always reflective, has
become even more so since his retirement. During his time on
the job, he saw it all. I value his wisdom and insight and often
seek his advice.

"They ought to put the state patrol in charge," he says.

"What?"

"The governor ought to put you guys in charge."

"Well," I say, "it doesn't work that way. Besides, I don't know what we'd do if we were in charge."

"Something different," my father-in-law says.

☆

Day five. Day *five*. It's hard to wrap my mind around that number. Five straight days of unrest and uncertainty. The only thing I'm sure of is that the protests will continue tonight. I expect a larger crowd and a more significant police presence.

At the command post, rumors fly through the room: *The governor is calling in the National Guard, declaring a state of emergency, imposing a curfew.*

Like everyone else here, I'm on edge—pacing, sipping at a can of soda, drifting outside, then back inside again. At one point, I cruise up to West Florissant to see for myself what's happening. As I drive, I battle a mix of feelings—from frustration to uselessness. Everyone seems to want to draw a stark division between the two groups on the streets—protesters and law enforcement—and assign a fixed value to the distinction: *good versus evil.*

Of course, it's not that simple.

The protesters come from a wide swath of humanity, including people with a cause—angry, impatient citizens determined to express themselves peacefully; people who feel forgotten, unseen, and unheard; people who want to show their support for the people of Ferguson and the Brown family; and a stream of state and national officials, here for a variety of reasons.

Mixed in and among the demonstrators, walking alongside them, are reporters from the national news networks; cable news outlets such as CNN, MSNBC, and VICE News; major news magazines and newspapers; and Internet news sources such as the *Huffington Post* and the *Daily Beast*. And then there are those who *call* themselves members of the media—some even waggle homemade press passes—but who don't represent actual media outlets; they simply own cell phones and feverishly post photos on Twitter, Facebook, or Instagram.

Finally, there are the *rioters*—people enraged by the Michael Brown shooting who feel compelled to wreak mayhem, damaging or destroying whatever building, obstacle, or person stands in their way—and the *looters*, opportunists who use the unrest as an excuse to take things that don't belong to them.

One cannot paint the other side—law enforcement—with a single brushstroke either. Officers from more than fifty law enforcement agencies have descended on Ferguson, including those who have come on their own. This wide array of officers arrives with differing levels of training and experience. Given the tension here, I'm not sure that *more* equals *better*. I don't believe we're accomplishing anything by bringing in more force, by becoming more militarized.

I hear horror stories. I hear about nerves fraying and adrenaline-fueled aggression. I hear about police smashing camera equipment, running people off the streets, screaming profanities at protesters, arresting innocent people who don't disperse as quickly as they demand, and even hauling off and arresting members of the media because they can't distinguish them from the protesters.

But in contrast to one report that says we are arresting *only* peacekeepers or members of the media, we have also been arresting rioters and looters who vandalize businesses and attack other people, including the police. It's fair to say we're not batting 1.000. It's also fair to say we're not batting .000.

★

Journalists need to write, record, and broadcast this story. The younger ones, the upstarts from the lesser-known outlets competing with the larger national news organizations, elbow their way to the front, fighting for their space, taking more chances. I want them to get the story, but I fear for their safety.

We warn them. Officers shout through bullhorns and loudspeakers, "Clear the street!" and I hear a voice in the crowd respond, "I'm a journalist. I need to be here."

Then I hear, "I'm telling you to *clear the street*," followed by a journalist defiantly saying, "I'm here in a peaceful way, and I'm not leaving."

And then the officers' instincts kick in. They charge, swarm, and force the journalist to leave.

I understand the police perspective. But I also respect the journalists and see that they, too, want their voices to be heard.

All of us—citizens, protesters, journalists, police—need to talk to each other.

Even more, we need to help each other.

But right now, on this Wednesday night, we face off against each other—police and protesters—two lines formed in defiance and anger.

We won't get anywhere this way.

We'll just be right back here tomorrow.

★

Night falls on day five. The protesting escalates. Rioters emerge from the crowd. They throw bottles, rocks, Molotov cocktails. They fire guns. Law enforcement reacts. Voices crackle through bullhorns.

"Go home or face arrest!"

One . . . two . . . three . . .

The streets erupt with smoke bombs, flash grenades, and tear gas. And then the searing *ping-ping-ping-ping* of the sound cannon, a Long Range Acoustic Device (LRAD) that works like a sonic machine gun to the brain.

Ping-ping-ping-ping . . .

It doesn't stop.

People cover their ears, screaming, crying, choking on the smoke and tear gas, running . . . the world a circle . . . nobody able to find their way out . . .

Flash grenades scuttle across the asphalt and into neighboring yards. Fires burn where Molotov cocktails have landed. Voices wail.

"I'm not doing anything!" someone yells.

The cops respond: *"CLEAR. THE. STREET."*

☆

We sit at the command post, trapped in a circle of despair.

A long silence.

"This isn't working," somebody says.

Jon Belmar buries his face in his hands. After a moment, he lifts his head. His eyes have turned the color of ash.

"We're going to go home and think about something different to do tomorrow," he says.

☆

The fear. The anger. The pain.

It all melds together and becomes a smell.

It's on me.

All over me.
I smell it on my clothes.
I can't rub it off.
I can't wash it away.
It seeps out of my pores.

I pray.
Please, God, I ask you . . . please . . . give us a different morning.

I lie in bed.
I think of my hero.
My dad.
If I had a problem, I went to him. He always had the answer.
He was a policeman.
He would know what to do.
Dad, what do I do?
I wish he could tell me.

☆

Sleep won't come. I stare at the ceiling. I slam my eyes closed.
I try to slow my breathing and shut everything out of my mind.
I breathe.
In.
Out.
Again.
I open my eyes and I see . . . Ferguson . . . West Florissant.
Crammed with people—thousands of people—marching, shout-
ing, fists in the air. They see me and slowly start walking toward
me. Advancing, they come closer . . . closer . . . I blink, furiously,
because . . .

They have no faces.
Nobody has a face.
I can't see any faces.

DAY 6

THURSDAY, AUGUST 14, 2014
DAYLIGHT

A DIFFERENT MORNING

Step right up, be a man;
You need faith to understand.
So we're saying for you to hear,
"Keep your head in faith's atmosphere."

EARTH, WIND & FIRE
"KEEP YOUR HEAD TO THE SKY"

ON THURSDAY MORNING, I speak to members of student government at Riverview Gardens High School, the same high school I attended and where the poorer residents of Ferguson go.

I speak to twenty-five students, the majority of them African American. They express confusion and deep emotion. One young woman sitting in the back bursts into tears. For days she has felt nothing but pain and loss. I tell her I understand and that I share her feelings. I pass out my business card and invite the students to call or e-mail me at my office anytime. I then ask each of them to write me a letter about how these days in Ferguson have had an impact on them and how they feel. I tell them to write from their hearts and not hold anything back; that after these days have passed—after this crisis is over—I will read their letters to the troopers who have been assigned here. I remember my prayer from last night and share my words with them.

"Today is going to be different," I say. "I know it's going to be different."

⭐

As I leave the high school and head to the command post, my boss, Bret Johnson, calls me.

"What's up, Bret?"

"The governor is coming to town. He's holding a press conference."

This can mean only one thing. He's making some changes.

"What's this about?" I ask.

"I don't know," Bret says. "The colonel will be there, and he wants all of us there too."

"Who else?"

"Everybody," Bret says. "The mayor of St. Louis City, the county executive of St. Louis County, Belmar . . . *everybody*."

"This involves us," I say. "It has to. We're the only agency the governor leads."

"I know nothing," Bret says.

I'm pretty sure I believe him.

Bret gives me the time and place for the governor's press conference.

"On my way," I say.

We meet in a small community room at the University of Missouri, St. Louis. Clearly the governor's staff has spread the word that he will be making a major announcement, because members of the national and local media jam into a larger connecting room where the governor will hold the actual press conference. I drift into the smaller room and see Jon Belmar standing by himself. He looks as if he hasn't slept in days. I walk over to him.

"Last night," he says, shaking his head.

"I know," I say. "The worst night yet."

We both go silent, waiting. Belmar nods toward the governor. "What's he going to say? What do you hear?"

"I just heard he's going to make some changes," I say. "I don't know what that means."

"No idea?"

"None."

After another brief, awkward silence between us, we turn our attention to Governor Jay Nixon—tall, white haired, and distinguished looking, but appearing anxious or even nervous— who stations himself at the front of the room. He rifles through some papers, pauses to gather himself, and then speaks rapidly.

"Over the past several days, we have all been deeply troubled by this crisis, as the pain of last weekend's tragedy has been compounded by days of grief and nights of conflict and fear."

I shift my weight and try to focus on the words in the governor's blistering delivery.

"What's gone on here over the last few days is not what Missouri's about. It's not what Ferguson is about. This is a place where people work, go to school, raise their families, and go to church—a diverse community, a Missouri community. But lately, it's looked a little bit more like a war zone. And that's unacceptable."

The governor peers at the paper in front of him and then looks up. He speaks so quickly now that he doesn't appear to breathe.

"Literally, the eyes of our nation and the world are on us. In order for that important process of healing and reconciliation to begin, we need to address some very immediate challenges. That's why today I'm announcing that the Missouri Highway Patrol, under the supervision of Captain Ron Johnson, who grew up in this area, will be directing the team that provides security in Ferguson."[1]

I feel . . . *staggered*.

I did not know about this. I did not expect it. I had no inkling, no insight, no warning.

I feel my pulse rocket and my mouth go dry.

The governor just put me in charge.

What does this mean?

What am I supposed to do?

It suddenly occurs to me that now I am not only in charge but have also just replaced Jon Belmar, who is standing right next to me. I turn to him and read his expression—a mixture of shock and anger.

"Hey, Jon," I say. "I had no idea."

He stiffens and his stare bores right through me—and then he turns away.

He doesn't believe me.

I suppose if our roles were reversed, I wouldn't believe him either.

I want to say something else to him, but no words come.

The governor finishes his speech. He thanks the members of law enforcement and emphasizes the need for understanding and healing in Ferguson. Within seconds, I find myself swept up into a group of people I don't know, and then I'm face-to-face with the governor. He shakes my hand.

"The colonel and I believe you're the guy for the job."

"Yes, sir."

"If you need anything—"

His voice trails off. He seems on edge, as if he's about to burst. I would bet he hasn't had much sleep lately—like the rest of us.

"Thank you, sir," I say.

"When we get in there with the media, I'll basically repeat what I just said, and then I'll introduce you."

"That sounds fine."

A member of the governor's staff materializes in front of me. He nods and presses a dark-colored binder into my hands.

"Congratulations," he says, looking down at the binder. "We wrote a statement for you. The governor wants you to read it at the press conference. It's short."

"Okay," I say, still trying to grasp what is happening.

"Do you want to look it over?" the staffer asks. When I blink, confused, he adds, "The statement."

"Oh. Sure. Yes."

I open the binder and glance at the typed statement. All I see is a jumble of words, a blotch of letters swimming on a white page. I cannot fathom their meaning.

"Are you good with it?" the staffer says.

"Yes. It's fine."

"The governor wants you to stand behind him at the press conference."

"Great," I say.

The next thirty minutes evaporate, and I find myself being shuttled along with the same group of people, including the governor, from the smaller room to a larger one cluttered with cameras, boom microphones, and members of the media. I follow the governor up a few steps onto a stage. He moves to a podium and for the next four minutes repeats the same speech he delivered a few minutes ago. He talks about making a change and the need for healing and reconciliation. He praises the Missouri State Highway Patrol, and then he introduces me, the new head of security for Ferguson. As the governor turns toward me, I step forward to the podium, flip open the binder, and begin reading.

The statement floats out of my mouth, but I have no idea what I'm saying. I speak by rote, by reflex—the words well crafted yet canned, uncontroversial; necessary but generic. Certainly not *me*.

I know I say something about breaking "this cycle of violence" and "how important it is that Ferguson has confidence in law enforcement," but I really don't comprehend the words that are crossing my lips. When I finish the last sentence, I look up, mutter "thank you," and step back behind the governor. The entire speech takes just under a minute.

As Charles Dooley, the St. Louis County executive, steps to the podium, I close my eyes and try to gather myself. I need to find my bearings. I need to breathe. I need to grab hold of this moment. I think about the words I just read and feel as if I've lost an opportunity. I should have said something in my own words. I should have spoken from my heart. The governor appointed *me*. The people—the country—should have heard from me. I vow to always speak for myself from now on, for better or worse. I open my eyes, knowing that I will have another chance. I believe in second chances. We all must believe in second chances.

My second chance comes a few minutes later.

Back at the podium, responding to questions from the press, Governor Nixon prepares to take one last question. He points to a local reporter named David.

"I'd still like to hear from Captain Johnson what he says he's going to do different tonight," David says.

The governor whips around toward me and steps to the side. I walk to the podium and nod at the reporter.

"So, Captain," he says in a voice that sounds both skeptical and challenging, "I was wondering, what are you going to do differently tonight? Are you still going to roll in there with armored vehicles and police in full body gear or have a different appearance?"

"We're going to go back and assess—"

I stop myself.

I sound like a robot, as if I'm quoting from some kind of nonexistent riot-control manual.

I start again. I speak slowly, and this time I speak from my heart.

"We're going to start from today," I say. "We're not going to look back in the past."

And then, finding the reporter's eyes, I add, "When we talk about boots on the ground, *my* boots will be on the ground."

I remember now that we have received word of several members of the clergy leading a march this afternoon down West Florissant to the remains of the QuikTrip.

I know what I have to do. I will walk with those people as if I belong with them, as if I am one of them.

The words tumbling out, I say, "Actually, I plan on walking to the QuikTrip, which has been called Ground Zero, and meeting with the folks there myself tonight."

The moment I say this, the atmosphere shifts in the room. The air crackles. I feel a low-level hum. I don't hear it; I feel it.

"We are going to have a different approach," I say, "the approach that we are in this together."

And then I tell the people gathered in front of me—the

assembled law enforcement, public officials, and members of the media—about speaking to the students at Riverview Gardens High. I tell them about the young woman who cried. I tell them about suggesting that the kids write letters to me that I will share with troopers after these days are over.

And I tell them about my prayer.

"Like I do each and every night, I pray for a different morning," I say. "Today is going to be a different day for our community. . . . We're going to make a change today."[2]

☆

The press conference ends and a throng of city, county, and state officials pummel me with handshakes and good wishes. They repeat, *You've got my support—anything I can do*, over and over, as if on a loop. The governor pulls me aside, grips my hand again, and says, "You did great in there. I'm here if you need me. Good luck." And then he disappears.

I crane my neck in search of Chief Belmar, but he, too, has vanished. For a second I feel abandoned, on my own, but then another wave of people escorts me outside and hustles me into a truck with several troopers. Some of them murmur their congratulations; others say nothing.

I can't tell if they're looking *at* me or *past* me. Both, maybe. It occurs to me then that I have to show these troopers leadership. Confidence. At the moment, though, I can't say I *feel* confident. Everything feels unreal. As the governor said, the nation is watching Ferguson. What he didn't say was that the nation—including the troopers in this truck—would now also be watching *me*. Somehow, though, I push beyond my uncertainty. I have to.

As incredible as it feels, I know in the deepest part of me—in my soul—that I am ready for this. It's almost as if I've been preparing for this moment my whole life. I can acknowledge the momentousness of this—for me, for all of us—but I can't allow it to weigh me down. I simply have to move us forward.

"We're going to that march," I say to the troopers in the truck. "I'm going to support the clergy." I pause and then add, "It's the right thing to do."

Silence.

As we drive toward Ferguson, nobody says a word. The silence in the truck becomes stifling. I decide to call Lori, this being the only time I may have for hours to tell her the news.

"Hey," I say when she answers. I cup my cell phone, trying to keep my voice low, knowing that everyone in the truck is listening—and no doubt judging me. I realize that they will be judging everything I do from now on.

"The governor's made some changes," I say to Lori, clamping down the emotion I suddenly feel rising in my voice. "He put me in charge."

"He did *what*?"

"Yeah," I say, lowering my voice even more. "That's right."

"Why?"

Truthfully, this is not the response I was hoping for from my wife.

"Well—"

Of course, I had expected her to validate the governor's decision and pump me up. But Lori, being brutally honest—and scared for my safety, I suddenly understand—blurts out the first word that jumps into her mind, the same question I'm asking myself: *Why?*

I can't answer that question.

But I have to move past it.

The question doesn't matter.

I am in charge.

It's on me.

But Lori has a thousand follow-up questions.

"I'm just wondering, because this is so unexpected. Did the governor explain how he arrived at the decision? It's a big deal—"

"It's funny," I reply. "Your dad actually said we should be put in charge—"

"Did the governor consider anyone else? You're qualified, of course, the *most* qualified, but, specifically, *why?* Did he go into his reasons? Did he offer any details?"

I want to answer all her questions, and I will, or at least try to, but not now—not in the center of the silence and scrutiny of the troopers riding solemnly along with me. I love her inquisitiveness and concern, and I feel myself smile, but I have to deflect these questions.

"So, yes, that's right, he's made that change. We're on our way to Ferguson right now. I'll call you later, okay?"

"Okay." Lori pauses. "Ron—?"

"Yes?"

"Be safe."

☆

We continue driving, and still nobody says a word. I start to realize that the governor's putting me in charge came as a shock to the troopers, as well as to me. I don't know whether they accept me. But I can't dwell on that—or the *why.* I only know that once we get to Ferguson, I'm going to walk with the protesters. That will be my new tactic. My plan. And by doing this, I will already be instituting a radical change.

Still, I wonder . . .

Will the troopers walk with me, or will I walk down that road alone?

I close my eyes and rub the bridge of my nose as memories of the first time I was ever put in charge flood into my mind.

★

I am ten years old.

I wear an orange strap across my chest.

I am the school crossing guard.

I stand on the corner, and when I see that it's safe, I spread my arms and wave kids across the street.

Kids wait for my signal.

I feel a sense of authority and responsibility.

In my mind, I'm helping to get them safely to school and back home. Kids respect me. I feel that. That's new. Different. They don't tease me anymore. They don't call me names. I don't hear the word.

It helps that I have a friend, my next-door neighbor, Jeff. He's two years older, and his dad races cars.

When we first moved into the neighborhood, Jeff ignored me; but then I found out he hadn't spent much time around black people.

Jeff parents and mine never really interacted—nothing more than a nod when they saw each other. But Jeff and I started talking one day, and before long we were hanging out together and playing in his backyard after school and on weekends.

One day, Jeff invites me to go with his family to one of his dad's car races. I can tell that my mother has concerns, but she lets me go. At the racetrack, Jeff and I walk around the pit area, where the crews service the cars before and during the races. Everyone knows Jeff because of his dad, and people stop and talk to him. Every person I meet—every face I see—is white. At one point, a guy Jeff is talking to tilts his head toward me and asks, "Who's this?"

"This is Ron," Jeff says. "He's my friend."

★

By the time I entered junior high, several more black families had moved into the neighborhood, and life had gotten easier. My high school years at Riverview Gardens were typical and unremarkable. I played trumpet in the school band. I ran track. I made the varsity football team and played tight end. I was a decent player at a wiry 170 pounds, but that didn't mean much my senior year when we lost every game. I dated my share of girls and went to prom. I graduated from high school and went on to earn a degree in criminal justice at a local college. I checked all the boxes.

Before I knew it, I was edging toward twenty-three years old, working at UPS, with my career on the rise. I had moved up from working the loading dock to part-time supervisor, but I felt stuck, restless. Even though I had a good job and worked with some good people, every day when I went to work, my spirit felt crushed. As I pored over packing lists and employee shift schedules, six words kept screaming through my head: *I want to be a policeman.*

Still.

Always.

Since forever.

One day, after practically losing my mind at work, I called the

Missouri State Highway Patrol recruiting office when I got home. I told the officer who answered the phone that I was interested in becoming a trooper. I chose state trooper over other divisions of law enforcement because I didn't want to be confined to a particular area. I wanted to police the entire state. The officer arranged for a recruiter to come to my house the very next day.

The recruiter interviewed me, met my dad, and told us enthusiastically that the MSHP was committed to signing up more minorities. A few days after my home interview, I drove to the Patrol's troop headquarters in St. Louis County to take the first round of my official entrance exam: the written test.

Wearing pressed slacks, a blue blazer, and a tie, I entered a large room where everyone else I could see was wearing blue jeans and T-shirts. Some were even in shorts. At first I thought, *Ron, you look like a big nerd.* But then I said to myself, *No, you look properly dressed.* My parents had taught me the importance of making a good first impression—even when I'm just taking a standardized test in a room with fifty other people.

Looking back, I believe I dressed up that day for another reason. I dressed up out of respect for law enforcement.

As I nervously opened the first page of that test, I felt a sudden sense of awe for the blue, for the badge.

I passed the written test without a problem.

Next I had to take a physical fitness test—a mere formality. I was a former high school athlete and had kept myself in good shape ever since. I had spent months working on the loading dock at UPS. I had no worries about passing the fitness test.

I failed the fitness test.

A tall, sullen-faced trooper ran a group of us through several exercises. One exercise required us to squeeze a small rubber grip with a built-in meter that measured hand strength. When it was my turn, I grabbed the device and slowly applied pressure.

The meter barely moved.

I failed—along with another guy I knew casually, a massively muscled former college linebacker.

"You guys didn't pass," said the trooper administering the test.

I was so stunned that I had difficulty forming words.

"I can't believe—"

"You can always try again. Come back in six months."

My body deflated. I slumped toward the door, my legs barely moving. I had never felt so defeated.

As I stepped into the hallway, I heard the trooper say, "Hey. Come back in here for a minute."

I turned, but he was talking to the linebacker.

"You're a big guy," I heard the trooper say. "You had to be doing something wrong. There's no way you couldn't make that meter move." Then, speaking out of the corner of his mouth, he said, "You want to try it again?"

"Sure."

Wait, what?

He had my full attention now.

That's bias, pure and simple, plain as day.

The trooper was making an assumption about the linebacker—and about me—just by the way we looked. The linebacker may have been bigger, but who's to say he was any stronger?

I propelled myself back through the doorway, nearly knocking the linebacker over.

"Sir, if he can try it again, can I?"

The trooper hesitated, but he had been caught.

"Fine," he said.

The trooper handed the device to the linebacker and whispered urgently under his breath, "You have to squeeze the handgrip really tight and right away. Don't press it gradually. You have to give it a jolt."

The linebacker nodded, took the handgrip, and squeezed it hard and fast. The needle on the meter moved to the right.

"I knew you could do it," the trooper said. Then he looked at me. "You sure you want to try it?"

Sometimes, even when you *deserve* equal treatment, you have to fight for it.

I smile. "Yes, I'd like a second chance too."

I took the handgrip from him and squeezed it immediately. The needle on the meter fluttered and then sprung all the way to the far right-hand side.

I grinned at the trooper. "I believe I pass."

"I guess so," the trooper said.

"Thanks for giving me a second chance," I said. "You won't regret it."

The next step in the process was boot camp—the most grueling, debilitating, mind-numbing half year of my life. (The linebacker, incidentally, was not selected.) For six months, the training sergeants screamed at us, criticized us, and belittled us. When it came to marksmanship, I ranked lowest in my class, which made me the target of merciless taunting from my superiors. As each day ground into the next and every day melded into a blurry, bad dream, I never doubted that I would gut it out—and I did, surviving at times on sheer determination and pride.

During that six-month ordeal, I learned a valuable, lifelong lesson: It doesn't matter how strong you are physically. What matters is your inner strength. Your spirit. Your will. Your heart.

In fall 1987, I graduated from the academy and officially joined the ranks of the Missouri State Highway Patrol. To celebrate, my parents threw me a party—nothing elaborate, just family and a few friends gathered for food and drinks in the party room in our finished basement.

I mingled with the guests for a while, and then my dad took me aside and said, "Go upstairs and put on your uniform."

I felt like I was eight years old and my dad was telling me to put on my Halloween costume or my Little League uniform for everyone. But I caught the look in his eye, and I knew it was more than that.

"Okay," I said.

After a few minutes, I came down the basement stairs wearing my full dress uniform. My dad took a few steps toward me and stopped, locked in place, his eyes glued on me. I have never seen such . . . *pride*. He froze for a moment, and then his bottom lip began to tremble. I hugged him, both of us trying valiantly to hold back our tears.

★

All these years later, riding in that truck on the way to Ferguson—as head of security in the aftermath of the Michael Brown shooting—a vision of my dad flashes before my eyes. I see his gaze riveted on my face, his eyes filling up with tears, brimming with pride. I only wish I could walk down those basement stairs again and see my dad one more time.

★

I received my first assignment as a newly minted Missouri state trooper: South St. Louis County, a middle-to-upper-class, majority-white community. I worked eight-hour shifts—days at first, and then nights. Eventually I would work alone, but in the beginning another trooper accompanied me in the field, training me.

Early on, we worked a horrible fatal crash involving a motorcycle. The trooper told me I would have to inform the wife of the motorcycle rider that her husband was dead.

I was twenty-four years old.

As we headed to the bank where the young wife worked, the trooper tried to prepare me by predicting the questions the woman might ask. As he talked, I found it hard to focus. I felt overwhelmed with sadness.

The trooper and I walked into the bank and found the manager. We asked if we might speak to the woman privately.

"We have some bad news," the trooper said. "It's about her husband."

We didn't have to say any more. The bank manager set us up in an empty office, and the trooper and I waited, standing uncomfortably in the middle of the room, holding our hats.

After a few minutes, the bank manager returned with the young wife. When she saw us, her face caved in. I began to sweat. Rivulets of perspiration slid from my forehead, pouring down my cheeks and onto my neck. The young woman gripped the edge of a desk, and a whimper escaped from her lips. She started to cry.

I cleared my throat. "I'm sorry," I said. "Your husband—"

I couldn't find any more words. But the woman didn't need to hear anything else right then. She shook her head furiously and began to sob.

I felt so helpless.

I was supposed to be this . . . *policeman* . . . this symbol of strength. Instead, I felt as if my legs were about to give out.

The woman clutched herself, tears pouring down her face.

I looked at the trooper standing next to me. He had not trained me for this. He hadn't given me any protocol for dealing with grief.

What do I say to her?

How do I comfort her?

Do I touch her shoulder?

Do I hug her?

I searched for answers in his eyes.

He looked away, his eyes clouded, distant.

By instinct, I reached out and put my arms around the young woman.

"I'm so sorry," I said.

She sniffled and nodded, trying to find strength. And then she howled, her pain bellowing forth all at once in a squall of pure grief.

I had nothing else to say. I held her until she finally found enough strength to let me go.

"You're kind," she said as the bank manager gently led her away.

★

Once my training period was completed, I patrolled the highways alone, working accidents, watching for speeders, lane-to-lane weavers, and worse. I arrested drunk and reckless drivers, and occasionally criminals. Our cars weren't equipped with partitions between the seats, so the people I arrested rode up front with me. The days flew by—every day different, every day new.

One time when I stopped a guy for speeding, I approached

the car and could see that he was very agitated. He was wearing a suit, with his tie loosened and askew, and he was drumming his fingers on the steering wheel, repeatedly checking his watch.

"You know why I'm stopping you?" I asked.

"Yes, sir. I know I was speeding." He fastened his eyes on me. "Officer, my wife and I are trying to conceive a child. I'm racing home from work because she's ovulating. We only have a small window."

I coughed to keep myself from laughing.

"I don't know if you're telling me the truth, but that's the best story I've ever heard. Go home. Just slow down to make sure you get there. And good luck."

I patted the side of his car.

☆

I never wrote a poor person a ticket. I know what it feels like to struggle. I know what it means to have to choose between feeding your family and heating your home. I believe—with all my heart—that every good policeman must have compassion. Empathy. We need to feel for each other. We need to learn to lead with our hearts.

One winter when I was about twenty-five years old, I pulled over a car that was speeding and slowly approached it. I saw there was a family inside—the dad behind the wheel, the mom in the passenger seat, and three little kids in the back. The kids were wearing clothes that seemed shabby, and all three were without shoes, even though the day had turned bitterly cold. They were sharing a box of cereal.

I asked for the dad's license and registration. As I looked it over, I heard the wife say—not in anger, but in frustration, "I told you to slow down. Now you got a ticket. How are we going to pay for a ticket?"

I caught the dad glaring at his wife. His look said, *You're embarrassing me in front of this policeman. Please stop and let me talk to him.*

I walked back to my cruiser to run the plates and make sure the license and registration checked out. As I returned to their car, the cold wind kicked up, biting my face. I indicated for the dad to roll down his window and then handed him back his license and registration.

"You have a nice family," I said.

The mom and dad just stared at me.

"Looks like you're having a tough time. If I give you a ticket, it will only make things worse." I paused. "You do need to slow down."

"Yes, officer," the man said. "I will."

"Wait," the wife said. "You're not giving us a ticket?"

"Not today," I said. "Have a good rest of your day. And remember: Slow down."

The dad knew he was in the wrong, and he knew he'd been caught. But giving this family a ticket would only have made their lives harder. They definitely would have struggled to pay the two-hundred-dollar fine, and they may not have been able to afford it at all without sacrificing something else, something they needed for their family. Plus, a moving violation may have required a court appearance, which could've cost the dad a day of work. By being treated with compassion—by having a positive interaction with a police officer—these people might start to formulate a different opinion about police in general.

I knew I had pledged to enforce the laws. That's what "the

book" says. But the book didn't see those three little kids without shoes in the middle of winter and the panic on their parents' faces. I believe the book needs a revision, a second draft. It should be rewritten with a greater emphasis on empathy.

Law enforcement and civilians—we're in this together. We have to abide by the law, but we also have to look out for each other.

☆

Our truck arrives in Ferguson. As we head toward the beginning of the protest march, I scan the streets. We drive past small crowds of people, and then gradually the crowds grow larger. I hear jeering, taunting, shouts of "Don't shoot!"—and I feel a crackle and hum in the air. I picture a lit fuse. It's daylight now, but already I'm thinking, *I dread the night.*

I look at the troopers riding in the back. They have been quiet since we left the press conference, and their faces are blank, impassive. I don't know what they're thinking, but I can't focus my energy there. I can't think of anything to say to erase any doubts or concerns they have. I know that troopers respond to confidence, to certainty. I am certain of only one thing: I am going to walk down that street.

I close my eyes as we ride. I breathe slowly. I open my eyes as the truck pulls over near a line of damaged and looted stores on West Florissant. As the troopers climb out of the truck, I hesitate a moment to gather myself . . . and another flash of memory hits me.

☆

I am twenty-five years old, patrolling Jefferson County, a rural—and mostly white—area of St. Louis with a reputation for being less than friendly to black people.

One day I work a car accident involving a young woman. She doesn't appear seriously hurt, but she seems shaken and possibly in shock. I calm her as best I can. I summon an ambulance, but I'm told it may take some time for the paramedics to arrive. I offer the young woman some water and promise to stay with her. After a few minutes, a late-model car pulls up and an older white man gets out. He walks quickly to the young woman—his daughter. A little while later, a tow truck arrives, followed by the ambulance. As the paramedics examine the young woman, the father comes over to me.

"You never left," he says.

"I wanted to make sure the ambulance got here all right and that your daughter was okay."

"I'm very grateful," the man says. He dips his head and goes back to tend to his daughter.

The next day, the young woman's father phones me at work, asking if I can meet him at a specific spot on the highway.

I drive to the designated place and find the man waiting for me. As I pull over, the man waves to me and returns to his car. He comes back with a plate covered in aluminum foil. He lifts the foil and I see that the plate is packed with barbecue—ribs, corn, potato salad, the whole works.

"I got up early this morning and barbecued just for you," he says, beaming. "I hope you like it."

"I don't know what to say. Thank you."

I take the plate from him, and we shake hands. I look at the food he cooked especially for me. His gift. His thank-you. He didn't give me money or something he bought at a store. He gave me a part of himself, something he made. This isn't just food; it is *him*. I feel incredibly moved.

✯

The memory dissolves and I suddenly see an image of Michael Brown, his soft, round face lit up in a smile. And then I see his mother's stricken face, his father's tortured eyes, and I think, *No matter what color we are, our children are precious to us.*

Our children are so precious.

✯

I am in charge now, I repeat to myself. *This is on me now. This is on me.*

Reality slaps me. I feel as if a large, impossibly heavy weight has begun pressing down on my chest. Emotionally, I feel like I'm flailing.

I have nowhere to turn.

My lips tremble and I start to pray.

"Please, God, let there be no blood on my hands. Let everyone— every police officer, every person on the street—be safe."

Please don't let there be blood on my hands.

DAY 6

THURSDAY, AUGUST 14, 2014
AFTER DARK

"I NEED ANSWERS"

To enter the fire is to be burned.

PHILIP LEVINE
"BURNED"

"LET'S GO TO THE MARCH."

I speak softly to the eight or nine troopers encircling me on the sidewalk. A few shift their weight uncomfortably. One clears his throat. Another coughs. For five nights, we've seen the police line up wearing riot gear—shields, camouflage, gas masks, bullet-proof vests—with military-style weapons at the ready and dogs restrained on leashes. Until now, no one has proposed that the police come out on the street, wearing just their blue uniforms. No one has suggested that we perform our security duties with no face guards, no gas masks, no vests, no riot gear at all.

But that's exactly what I'm proposing now.

Since leaving the press conference, I haven't stopped at the command post. I haven't even called the command post to ask for backup or to announce that I'll be marching with the protesters. I need to be on the street.

Speaking louder and with more purpose, I again say to the troopers standing around me, "Let's go to that march."

We hear that the protesters will gather at Chambers Road, then march down West Florissant past the remains of the QuikTrip, ending on Canfield Drive at the site of the Michael Brown shooting. I watch as the crowd forms and builds, their voices lifted and arms raised. People approach me. Some police officers shake my hand and congratulate me. People I've never met point at me and say, "Hey, there he is." Jake Tapper from CNN asks if he can interview me for a minute or so. He asks a couple of questions, including, inevitably, "Why did the governor choose you?"

"We all knew that we needed to try something different," I say. "I've also lived in this area for more than forty years. I know the people."

I tell him it's time for all of us across America to listen to what these protesters have to say. It's time to really *listen*.

★

Several days ago, after the second day of protests, I had asked my family to stay off social media because of all the inaccuracies reported there and the hatred I had seen posted, some of which was directed at me. Still, I absolutely understand the value of social media, and I accept its place in our world. People writing about and posting photos of the Michael Brown shooting are inflaming passions and bringing attention to Ferguson.

I also embrace the mainstream media. CNN and MSNBC, the *New York Times*, the *Washington Post*, and other news outlets have sent people to report and broadcast the protests, the violence, the looting, the rioting, and the police response to it all. I understand that. I want that. But now I want the mainstream media to show a different response, a different type of police activity. I want people to see a police officer walking down this street.

In the mass of protesters, I find Pastor Traci Blackmon, a well-known figure in our community and one of the leaders of the upcoming march. I know Pastor Blackmon well enough to call her by her first name. We met through our kids and have become friends.

"Hey, Traci, how are you?"

We hug, and then we stand looking at each other for an uncomfortable moment.

"What can I do for you?" she asks.

"I'm here to march with you guys."

She nods. "I'd rather you not."

"Okay," I say, laughing. I assume she's joking, but then I realize she's dead serious. "Well, the governor has put me in charge of the security detail here in Ferguson."

"No," she says.

Again, it feels like she's joking, but I know she has just smacked me with a sharp dose of humility. Her no says, *Don't puff out your chest. Don't think you're somebody special.*

Then she says, "Congratulations."

"Thank you," I say, and an enormous feeling of inadequacy overcomes me. I step outside myself, and suddenly I feel so . . . small. I feel overwhelmed by the moment, lost in this new responsibility. I have never felt so confused, so unsure.

"Pastor Blackmon," I say, no longer speaking to her as my friend, but as a person of God, "I need to march for *me.*"

My eyes fill up.

"I have nothing else," I say.

I look directly at her, but I can't see her clearly. My tears shroud her in a haze. Her features shimmer.

"I'll march in the back," I say. "When we get close to the crowds, I'll step out and no one has to know I'm marching."

"No." She shakes her head gravely. "You can march, but I want you to march in front."

I feel it then.

A shift.

Like a jolt of electricity surging through me.

The moment rattles me. Stuns me. In this moment, it starts.

God has humbled me. I *feel* it. I *know* it. I know that from this moment on, I will be marching—tonight and for as long as it takes—as an instrument of God's grace, God's mercy, and God's power. I will be walking—and working—for *him*.

I'm no one special. I have no unique talent, no special gift. I'm just a man. But tonight God has a hold on my life.

★

I walk.

At first the crowd numbers a hundred people or so, but then the numbers swell—two hundred, three hundred, and then hundreds more. The energy around me changes from a negative, dangerous vibe to something pulsing, positive, even celebratory. I hear a local news reporter—standing on a street corner, holding a microphone—broadcasting to greater St. Louis that tonight the police are walking *with* the protesters—no riot gear, no gas masks. *Tonight*, the reporter says, *Ferguson feels . . . different.*

Like a scene out of the Bible, the sea of people in front of me separates as we make our way down West Florissant. I walk slowly, taking it all in, not quite believing what I'm seeing. Gradually, people close in to greet me, to encourage me, to walk with me. Not knowing what to expect, I swivel my head from side to side, cautious and vigilant at first. Car horns blare. People shout. Voices holler randomly, a mix tape of indistinguishable phrases. At some point the voices come together, shouting the same phrases, chanting a call and response, and then singing—in *harmony*. The protest becomes music.

Hands reach toward me. I touch them, grasp them, shake them, fist-bump them, slap five with them, touch them. Hands rub my arms, clasp my shoulders, pat my back. I walk into a tunnel of sound—shouting, music, street noise, bullhorns squawking— a deafening chorus echoing all around me. Something about this walk feels like a rally, like—dare I say the word—a *party*.

I don't know when I veer off from the march, but at some point I realize that I'm marching alone, except for three officers I've assigned to watch my back, who trail me, on the lookout for anyone who might toss a bottle or a rock, or do worse. Protesters fill the gaps between us and on all sides, reaching out, screaming my name.

"Captain Johnson!"

Even though the very air around me seems electric, slivers of doubt still swim in my mind.

I know I'm doing the right thing.

I know I am.

I am—right?

Sometimes when we most need an answer, when we need for God to show us if we're on track, he sends us a sign.

Just then a woman rushes out of the crowd and charges toward me. Before I can react—before anyone can stop her—she throws her arms around me and clings to me, holding me tight in her embrace. As she holds me, I hear her sobbing.

"Thank you," she says. "Thank God for you."

Then as quickly as she charged out of the crowd to hug me, she disappears into a mass of people who swallow her up. For a moment I wonder, *Did that just happen? Was she real?*

As I continue to walk, I can't get that woman off my mind.

Whatever her intention, she has shown me that I'm doing the right thing.

She has delivered the message.

I feel as if a weight has lifted off me. My steps feel lighter; my purpose feels more certain.

To me, that woman was like an angel.

☆

Months later, after life returns to a semblance of calm, I'm sitting in a sports bar with some friends after work, and a woman is suddenly standing at our table. I don't see her approach. It's as if she had materialized out of thin air.

She smiles and says, "Do you remember me?"

"I'm sorry, I don't."

"You hugged me during Ferguson."

"I did? Well, you know, I'm sorry, but I hugged a lot of people—"

"I was the first person you hugged. You were walking down the street. I ran out to you and embraced you. I was crying and I hugged you."

I remember her now. I remember that night—the first night I walked down West Florissant. In my mind's eye, I see her run out of the crowd and throw her arms around me.

"Yes," I say. "I recognize you now. Of course."

She lowers her head shyly. "I don't know if you've seen it, but at the St. Louis Art Museum there is a photograph of me hugging you."

"I haven't seen it. But I will."

"I'm very grateful for you, Captain Johnson."

"Thank you," I reply. "I have to tell you: I wasn't sure about my decision to walk down that street. But then you appeared and hugged me and thanked me, and I knew I was doing the right thing. I thought of you as an angel."

"Well," she says, her smile returning, "I just wanted to come over and say hello."

"I'm glad you did."

She turns to go.

"Wait," I say. "What's your name? I have to know my angel's name."

"Angela," she says. "My name is Angela."

☆

I walk for more than two hours. I walk up and down West Florissant, my blue uniform shirt soaked through with sweat. When I reach the site of the former QuikTrip, I turn back up the street and keep walking, and the crowd comes with me. I don't see any looting. I don't hear of any violence.

At one point as I walk, I hear a lone male voice shouting. At first I can't make out what he's saying—I can't hear his words—but I hear his pain.

"There's no one," he shouts. "No one at all."

I follow the sound of his voice. I track it. His voice comes louder, clearer, closer. He speaks in an almost hip-hop rhythm.

"I'm not scared of your gas. I'm not scared of your badge. I'm not scared of your stick. That means nothing to me. I need answers—tonight."

I find him then—a young man wearing a hooded sweatshirt, with a bandanna covering his face, revealing only his eyes. An outlaw. At least that's the image he seems to want to project. But when I focus on his eyes, I see fear and pain and rage and youth. I see innocence destroyed.

"Where is he?" he shouts to the crowd, not seeing me. "Why has this happened? Why are we out here?"

He sees me now.

"Answer me this," he says, his stance confrontational, his body thrust forward in defiance. "Why are we out here?"

"If I answer your question," I say calmly, "I want you to listen to me, and I will listen to you. But let's not scream at each other."

"You first."

"We're out here to *get* answers. If I had answers to give you, young man, I would."

I let this sink in.

"If I could give you those answers, I would, trust me, because then all of us would go home tonight. But I guarantee you that every night when I go home and then when I wake up, I'm looking for some of the same answers you've been looking for. I will continue to do that."

I pause for a moment and then speak to him quietly, as if we were the only two people on the street.

"I want you to continue to voice your opinion," I say. "But I want you to do it in a way that's peaceful. I don't want you to get into any confrontations with *anybody* out here. Because when I come out here tomorrow"—I lean in toward him—"I want to see you tomorrow."

The young man's eyes widen—in surprise, in shock, perhaps in connection.

"I also want you to go home tonight. I know that your mother wants you to come home; your father wants you to come home— or if you don't live at home . . . wherever you live . . . I want you to be safe . . . and I want you to have some answers."

He nods almost imperceptibly.

"I guarantee you that when these days are over and we're all back in our homes, the answers we are looking for today—the answers we're going to get—are going to make our lives a whole lot better. They're going to make our community better. We're going to rebuild our businesses. They will be rebuilt. I know they will. Our businesses are going to come back. We will create new businesses."

The young man digs in, his eyes narrowing suddenly.

"Why are you out here on the street—with those police?" he asks. "You're not even Ferguson, Mr. Johnson. You're a state patrol officer."

I draw myself up to my full height.

"Let me tell you something. I want to make this clear to every-body. I'm not speaking for Ferguson. I'm not speaking for the Missouri State Highway Patrol. I'm speaking for *all* the citizens of the state of Missouri. And I will be honest with you about what's right, and honest with you about what's wrong."

The young man tilts his head slightly, and when he speaks, his voice cracks with heartache: "I need *answers*, sir, for real."

He pulls down his bandanna.

A young man—his face round and full, pudgy, almost childlike, his eyes soft and wide and surprisingly caring—stands before me. He looks to be in his early twenties, about the same age as my son. I have an urge to hug him and tell him it will be all right, that everything is going to be all right.

"You need to speak for us," he says. "We need answers. Why did Mike go down in cold blood? Why are they waiting to put the video out? Why are these things happening now?"

Each question stabs me.

"Some of those things you're asking me," I say, "I don't have a *why*. I don't. But I want to tell you, when you say 'speak for *us*,' you know what *us* should be? I know you don't believe it today, but *us* should be *all of us*."

He sniffs. A man standing next to him, an older man I'm seeing now for the first time, rubs the young man's arm. A loving touch. A father's touch.

"*Us* should be all of us," I repeat. "Not separately. Not two counties. Not two Missouris. Not two United States. *All* of us."

"You talking about us as a whole," the young man says weakly.

"That's what I'm talking about," I say. "Us as a whole. Everybody. We're out here asking for change."

I reach out and rest my hand on his shoulder. I look into his eyes, and I see this young man—this former outlaw—fighting back tears.

And I feel *this* stronger than ever: In order for policing to work, we have to come into the community, talk to the people—just like this—and listen. We have to *listen*.

"We're going to get you some answers," I say to the young man, my hand gripping his shoulder. "I promise you."

But even as I make that promise, I don't know if I can ever answer those questions.

Why?

Why do these things keep happening?

That's what this young man needs to know.

That's what we *all* need to know.

☆

I keep walking, and people keep coming up to me. They come close—so close—and I hug them. I feel their shaking bodies. I hear their trembling voices. I taste their tears. Their pain moves into me, cuts me, sends a chill rippling through me.

Nobody would believe this, I think. *Nobody would understand.*

Not everyone wants me walking down this street. Not everyone out here welcomes me. People on both sides—civilian and law enforcement—think I have betrayed them. The police believe I have identified myself with the protesters, become one of them. When I approach a group of white police officers, they turn their backs on me. Later I make a point of walking right up to them, engaging with them and asking, "Hey, how's it going?" They grunt or give me one-word responses.

The protesters believe I belong with the police, and they want us off the street. They want to *own* the street. Some want to terrorize us, and their rage spills over.

People curse at me.

Someone yells, "Get out! Get away!"

I don't confront anyone. They have a right to say what they want. And I have the right to walk.

A man comes up alongside me and starts to walk with me.

"Yes, this is about Mike Brown," he says. "But this isn't just about Mike Brown. We're out here because of a lot of other things too."

I stop at the top of West Florissant, at the crest of the hill, and look down the entire length of the street. I've walked for at least two hours, and now I'm going to walk back.

Overall, I would call tonight a good night, a night of change. I feel uplifted. But as I look down the street in the gathering darkness, I realize I don't know what's happening down there. Maybe the bottles and bricks and Molotov cocktails will come out now. Do I have the courage to walk down that street again? I don't know. But I know I have the strength. And I know I will walk. I have to walk. I will walk into the night, into the dark, not knowing what lies ahead. But I know I have to take the journey. I have to *act*, not knowing where the journey will end.

I finally understand.

That is what you call *faith*.

Today has felt as long as *two* days. I drive home feeling both exhilarated and exhausted. But we have achieved something. We have taken a step forward.

"We had a good night," I whisper to Lori as I get into bed, knowing I still have to answer all her questions. "A very good night."

"A start," she says.

"A first step," I say.

I fall asleep believing that.

DAY 7

FRIDAY, AUGUST 15, 2014

"SAVE OUR SONS"

I said to the Lord, "I'm going to hold steady on to you,
and I know you'll see me through."

HARRIET TUBMAN

FRIDAY MORNING, before I have showered and dressed, my duty officer calls to brief me on what happened in Ferguson last night after I left. He describes several incidents, the most serious one involving people throwing rocks at police, hitting four officers. No one suffered a serious injury, the duty officer says.

"We finally had a good night," I say. "Just not a perfect night."

I spend the next hour making calls, checking in with command, and setting up a news conference—my first—at ten o'clock. I still haven't heard from Jon Belmar, and I have traded calls with Tom Jackson. As I finish shaving, Lori rushes into the bathroom.

"Hey," she says. "You'd better see this."

I head into the bedroom and see Tom Jackson on TV, beginning a press conference. I hadn't heard that he intended to talk to the press.

"I'm here to talk about two things," he says, wearing a white short-sleeve shirt, standing at a microphone. "First of all—the name of the officer involved in the shooting."

"What?" I say to the TV.

"And then . . . I'm going to be releasing information about a robbery that occurred on August ninth, immediately preceding the altercation and shooting death of Michael Brown."

I fear what he's about to say next.

"Don't do it, Tom," I murmur to the television set.

"What we're making available today are the dispatch records and the video footage of a robbery—a strong-arm robbery with use of force—that occurred at a local convenience mart."

"He's releasing the security camera video," I say, feeling my jaw starting to clench.

"You didn't know about this," Lori says—a statement, not a question.

"No idea," I say. "We explicitly told him not to."

"I won't be taking any questions here," Tom says to reporters gathered in front of him. "I want to give this information to you, let everybody digest it, and then later on—sometime after noon—we can get together again, and then I'll take questions."

"I guess I'll be taking plenty of questions at *my* press conference," I say.

"I just want to give you a little timeline of what happened on August ninth," Tom continues. He squints over his reading glasses, holding some pages from a yellow legal pad at arm's length as he reads. "From 11:48 to noon, the officer involved in the shooting was on a sick call . . . there was an ambulance present. At 11:51, there was a 9-1-1 call from a convenience store nearby . . ."

Tom follows his timeline until—suddenly flustered—he loses his place. After shuffling through his notes, he recovers and blurts out, "At 12:01 p.m., our officer encountered Michael Brown on Canfield Drive . . ."

Tom then jumps to 12:04—*after* the shooting occurred. That three-minute gap screams.

"A second officer arrived at the scene, immediately following the shooting," Tom continues.

"This serves no purpose," I say to Lori, my voice rising. "Now people will have even *more* questions."

Tom starts to explain how the information packets will be distributed, and then someone off camera appears to ask him a question. Tom pauses, apologizes, shuffles through his notes again, and says, "The officer who was involved in the shooting of Michael Brown was Darren Wilson. He's been a police officer for six years. He has had no disciplinary action taken against him. He was treated for injuries, which occurred on Saturday."[1]

People begin shouting all around Tom Jackson. They shout so loudly that I can't make out what they're saying. I finally hear someone ask him to repeat the officer's name and to spell it. After Tom does that, he announces that he will answer questions later and steps away from the microphone.

"I wanted him to give that video straight to the grand jury," I say.

Lori doesn't reply, but I can read her expression.

Why?

"This will not help the situation out there," I say.

I try to understand Tom's mind-set. I want to give him every benefit of the doubt. I don't believe he acted out of malice. I think he simply wanted to support his department. He wanted to document publicly that a strong-arm robbery had occurred and that the officer in question—his officer—had suffered injuries. But right now, on the screen, the Ferguson police chief doesn't look at all satisfied or vindicated. He looks bewildered. I wonder if he realizes he's made an error in judgment.

"He just poured fuel on the fire," I say to Lori.

★

On my way to the command post, I think about what I will say at my news conference. I drive slowly, cruising down West Florissant. I see a crowd gathering. I pull over, get out of my car, and walk over to the growing group of people. As I approach, they converge, surround me.

"I'm sure you guys saw the news," I say.

They erupt, their emotions overlapping, crashing into each other, a mix of outrage and confusion. I wait quietly, allowing them to settle before I speak.

"I just want to tell you—I knew nothing about that news conference. I had no idea he was going to give out the name and release that video."

"Why did he do it?" a young man asks.

"I don't know," I say. "I truly don't."

"Do you agree with it?"

I look at the young man's expectant face, and for a moment time stops. I feel as if I have stepped outside my body. I am not here. I see myself as a police officer caught between the line of law enforcement I stand with and the people on the street—the citizens I've pledged to protect—squeezed into some horrible middle where the very ground beneath my feet seems to be sinking.

"Do you think he should have done it?" the young man asks.

A hush falls over the crowd as every single person seems to lean in for my answer. They know they have forced me to make a choice: Am I with them or with the police?

I choose neither.

I choose honesty.

"Do you think he should have done it?"

"No," I say.

"That's just what you're telling *us*," another man says. "You're here now so that's what you say now."

"*No*," I say forcefully. "That's how I feel. If anybody asks me, I'm going to say the same thing. My words are going to be the same whether I'm talking to you or talking in front of a camera. My words and my beliefs aren't going to change. My truth is my truth."

More grumbling and comments arise that I can't hear. I don't know whether I've gotten through to them at all.

"I'll tell you what. I've got a news conference at ten o'clock. It's going to be up at the shopping plaza. If you doubt my honesty, you can come to the news conference and hear for yourselves. You're all invited."

Shouts, garbled sentences, and then someone says, "I'll be there!" Others follow with a chorus of shouted agreement.

I head back to my car, thinking that a few of them might actually come to the press conference.

I'm wrong.

They *all* come.

At the command post, I meet briefly with Ferguson police chief Tom Jackson. I try to speak calmly, but I can't tamp down my anger. I tell him I don't agree with his decision to release the video and announce the name of the officer. He explains that he was responding to a "sunshine request" for the materials, referring to a Missouri state law ensuring that government meetings and records are open to the public, in accordance with the Freedom of Information Act.

"I don't know about that," I say.

"Well, that's what I was told."

"It shouldn't matter, Tom," I say. "You have to think about the family first and then the effect the video will have on the protesters. I just came from West Florissant and talked to people out there. Releasing that tape has them upset. We finally had a good night. This is going to set us back."

"I didn't think about that," Tom says, looking genuinely pained.

"I know you wanted to protect your department," I say. "But what did this accomplish?"

"Ron, honestly, I didn't think it would have that response. I really didn't."

I believe him. But that's not the point. The damage has been done.

★

Minutes before the scheduled start of my news conference, I stand at the podium in the parking lot in front of the command post. Cameras and microphones from local and national media pack the area in front of me. I look across the parking lot and see the group of people I spoke to on West Florissant clustered behind a line of yellow evidence tape. The group has grown. To me, they seem far away, out of hearing distance.

Before I know it, I'm on the move. I step away from the podium and walk across the parking lot. Behind me, as if anticipating what I'm about to do, voices shout, "Wait a minute, you can't do that!"

Without stopping, I yell back at them, "I want everybody to hear me."

I walk until I'm standing across from the group of protesters, with the evidence tape swaying between us. Then, lifting up the tape to allow them to pass, I say, "Come on up closer so you can hear."

The protesters hesitate for less than a second, and then they begin to move forward, pushing closer to the podium and the assembled journalists. I'm not certain, but I think I see some people smiling.

⭐

Back at the podium again, I begin the press conference.

"Last night was a great night," I say. "A great night. There were no calls for service. We did not deploy tear gas. We did not have any roadblocks. We did not make any arrests. It was a good night. People were talking. People were inspiring each other. People were getting their voices out. And we were communicating a lot better."

As I continue with my remarks, a reporter breaks in with a question about whether the release of the officer's name and the video from the convenience store changed the dynamics of the situation.

"I think the release of the name is what was requested by the community," I reply. "And they've gotten that. I have not seen the video. I was watching the news this morning when I heard that it came out, so I have not seen that. So it would be hard for me to comment on that. I will try to get a copy—or be able to analyze—the packet that they have. This afternoon I will be walking back down to the QuikTrip. I will talk to the people there and explain what I see in the packet. And some of the questions that may have been unclear in the presentation this morning, I will try to make those clear."[2]

I back away from the podium to allow the next speaker to address the media and the crowd, but as I step to the side I sense it—an undercurrent of anger welling up in the crowd. It's laced with something that feels dark. A kind of hatred almost. Yes, *hatred*, directed at me.

After the press conference, the media and the crowd of protesters disperse. I step inside the command post and an officer approaches me. His face pulses red, and he corkscrews his lips. He eyes narrow in anger.

"You call last night a good night?" he says. "No. I'm wrong. You called it a *great* night."

"Compared to the other nights since the shooting, yes, it was a great night. We had no arrests—"

"Did you forget about *us*? People were throwing rocks. We got *pelted* by rocks."

"Nobody got seriously hurt—"

"Four officers got hit. Four of your fellow officers."

"I know, but—"

"You weren't honest out there," he says, spewing the words. "You didn't tell the truth."

"Five percent of last night was bad," I say. "You think I should throw out the ninety-five percent good over the five percent bad?"

The officer stares at me. "You don't seem to care about us," he says. "You seem to care more about *them*."

There it is again.

Them.

These people.

The officer grunts and practically sprints to the coffee maker in the corner.

I look around the room. A few officers nod. Several more turn away. I grab my hat and head for the door. That's when I hear it, hurled at my back.

The word.

Burning into me.

As vicious and ugly as the first time I heard it at the all-white school when I was nine years old.

As the day goes on, it gets worse.

As if staging his own protest, Chief Jon Belmar has not yet made an appearance in Ferguson since the governor took away his command and put me in charge. Then I hear that the St. Louis County Police union rep has called a major newspaper to report that I lied during the news conference. I had said there were no major incidents Thursday night when in fact four officers were hit with rocks. I am immediately barraged by calls for clarification.

"Is the report true?"

"It is true," I admit.

"Why didn't you mention it at the press conference?"

"Because there *were* no major injuries. The officers were not seriously hurt. And the protesters did have a good night. I wasn't going to allow a few people to impact all the good that happened with the majority of the people. I wasn't trying to hide anything."

"But their rep said—"

"I know. I understand where you're coming from. But try to understand what I'm saying too."

I'm not sure they do.

Sometime later, I give my daily briefing to law enforcement, and I get hammered again.

"You didn't give all the facts," someone shouts. "Our guys got hit."

"It's a bigger picture," I say. "I'm not trying to go tit for tat."

The anger around my decision to keep silent about the officers who were hit by rocks, which has been bleeding into the moments of my day, feels as if it has begun to hemorrhage. Then I second-guess myself. I start to regret not mentioning those four officers. The regret stays with me, etched like a scar.

I regret that decision to this day.

★

I walk.

I walk alone.

Some police officers see me and turn away.

I draw myself up and keep walking.

The crowd builds. People walk with me. They encircle me. They shake my hand. They pat my back. I see some of the same people from last night. I look for the articulate young man who'd been wearing the hoodie and the bandanna mask. I don't see him, but I sense that he's here somewhere.

More people approach me. They talk to me.

"This here—being out here—gives me a reason," someone says.

"I hear you," I say, and I do. I truly do. Walking with me and with each other gives people a reason to stand. It gives them purpose. For some it may be the only purpose they have.

I see these people. I look at their faces and into their eyes, and I hear their voices. I know right then that nobody hears them. Nobody even tries.

I try to imagine how they feel—screaming for help and nobody hearing them. Their screams fading out into emptiness. Their pleas dying on their lips.

"I need you," they say. "Please hear me."

Their faces determined, their eyes expectant, their stride purposeful, they walk with me, hoping that maybe for the first time somebody will hear them, somebody will listen.

I listen. I hear them.

I have to. We all have to.

They see the change.

I feel it too.

A woman comes out of the crowd and races over to me, waving her cell phone.

"Captain Johnson, I want you to take a picture with my daughter. Please. I want her to know this moment and what we're doing."

I pose with her daughter, a little girl who looks about three years old. Her mother holds her up, and the little girl kisses me on the cheek. The mom takes the photo.

People thank me. They thank me for being here, for walking down the street with them, for telling them the truth about the video. They say they see my heart.

A woman around my age grabs my arm.

"Captain Johnson, please," she says, and then she starts to

cry. Tears rolling down her cheeks, she grips my arm tighter. "Save our sons," she says.

☆

I lead several officers into Ferguson Market & Liquor, the convenience store where the videotape came from. The tape shows Michael Brown in the store and the owner confronting him. I know that seeing Michael Brown alive—even in grainy security-camera footage—will enrage the community. I saw what looters did to the QuikTrip gas station. They torched it, burned it to a hollow shell. Now that the video has been released, I believe that looters will burn down this store as well. I have already started getting calls from people expressing their anger and warning me. I hear conversations on the street. The rage is coming. It's coming here. Releasing the video has put a bull's-eye on this store.

I stand with the owner and watch as people come and go. At one point, four young men walk in. I make eye contact with each of them. They meet my eyes and lock in. I see defiance and pure rage. One guy, perhaps the leader, breaks away from the group, goes to the counter, and buys a bottle of cognac. The store owner takes his cash and places the bottle into a brown paper bag. The young man pushes off from the counter and walks toward me. He takes the cognac out of the paper bag, pulls a red towel out of his pocket, and ties it around the neck of the bottle.

He stares at me.

"You know what that means?"

I do. He's showing me that he is going to make a Molotov cocktail.

He fixes a blazing stare on me for what seems like ten seconds, and then he brushes by me and leaves the store, the other guys trailing behind him.

I have received his message—his warning—but I can't do anything about it. He hasn't committed a crime. He's essentially told me that he's going to burn down the store, but I have to let him walk. I can't arrest him for buying a bottle of cognac.

I pull the store owner aside and explain what just happened.

"They're going to torch your store," I say. "They just told me as much. I want you to know what you will have to face. I can't say if it will be tonight or tomorrow or Sunday. It could be three, four o'clock in the morning. I don't know when they're going to come. But I know they are going to come."

"What about the cops?" the store owner asks. "What are you going to do?"

He tilts his head, mirroring the defiant look the young man who bought the cognac gave me.

"We are going to do what we can," I say, and then I gesture at his shelves. "But you need to take this stuff out of your store."

The store owner shrugs.

"No."

"No?"

"No. I don't have any help."

"I'll get you help."

I charge out of the store and round up a few officers. I ask them to wait outside while I go back into the store.

"I got a team of guys to help you," I tell the store owner. "Now let's move everything out. This could go down tonight."

The store owner sniffs. "I don't have a truck."

I bite my lip lightly and murmur, "I'll get a truck."

I make a call, and in less than fifteen minutes, an officer arrives with a truck. I go back inside the convenience store and tell the owner, "I got the truck. Now let's start moving everything out."

"No," he says. He leans back and another man steps forward. I had noticed this man before, but in the frantic past half hour of trying to round up guys and locate a truck, I didn't pay much attention to him. But now the store owner nods at the man.

"And you are?" I ask.

"My attorney," the store owner says.

"I see."

"I'm not moving anything out," the store owner says with a glance at his attorney. "I've got good insurance. I'm leaving everything here. Everything stays."

I can't believe this.

"Your call," I say.

In the parking lot, I gather the team of officers I've assembled. I ask one of them to return the truck. I ask the others to stay outside the store and wait. I hope they don't have to engage any rioters, but I know in my gut that tonight, tomorrow night, or early one morning, someone's coming to burn this place down.

☆

The calm before the storm.

That's what I feel.

An eerie stillness. And then a soft, warm breeze.

It feels so good against your face.

Makes you forget about the vicious storm blowing right behind it.

✮

I keep walking down the street. I keep interacting with protesters. I hear complaints about the video, but fewer than I expected, and no real outrage. Overall, I'd say we're having another good night. I return to the command post around eleven, feeling fairly positive about how the day has ended.

At eleven thirty, I get into my car and drive home from Ferguson. I get to bed just after midnight, feeling amped up and energized, murmuring a final thank-you to God for this very good day as I drift off to sleep.

Ten minutes later, an urgent call from the night commander jerks me awake. I kick off the covers, cup the phone so I don't wake Lori, and sprint into the bathroom.

The commander tells me that an angry mob had congregated outside the convenience store—their numbers quickly swelling, emotions burning hot. As the crowd began to rampage through the parking lot, the officers on duty called for more help. The night commander—seemingly not understanding what was happening—ordered the officers to leave. But they couldn't. A mob had cornered them—three or four officers, I'm not clear on the number—while looters attacked the store. The mob may have had guns, but they certainly had numbers. The night commander sent in two armored vehicles to break up the mob and allow the officers to escape the parking lot.

"Anybody hurt?" I say, reaching for my pants and my belt.

"No. I deployed tear gas."

I moan. "How many cans?"

"Just one."

"Do not deploy any more. *No more tear gas.* I'm on my way."

☆

Back in Ferguson now, I stand in front of an army. The commander has called for further assistance. Hundreds of officers—including four SWAT teams—assemble at the crest of the hill overlooking the stores on West Florissant. Down the street, looters have overrun the convenience store, and others have broken into the nearby Family Dollar store, smashing windows, carrying off merchandise, and destroying the building.

Then gunshots.

Snap . . . pop . . . crack . . .

I see rioters waving handguns and shooting them in the air.

I see rioters lighting rags on fire.

I see the night ablaze.

Behind me, two hundred police officers react as one. Without turning to face them, I can feel them stirring, psyching themselves up, preparing to engage.

They're ready to take it to the rioters. Ready to end this. Ready to disperse the crowd, round up the rioters, and arrest the looters.

Earlier today, I marched *with* the people.

Now the force behind me wants to march on them.

"What are we going to do?" a voice behind me shouts after a long few seconds.

"We need to go," another voice shouts. "We need to *go*."

I pivot slowly and take in all these officers gathered behind me. These troops, massed and ready. I can almost feel a collective ocean of adrenaline surging through them. And then I hear comments directed to me and about me—thrown at me—shards of doubt, anger, and mistrust. And maybe it's my imagination, but again I hear the word.

I give no signal.

My mind flits to the conversation I had after the news conference earlier today with the officer who called me out for not telling the media about the police who were hit with rocks. He challenged my honesty. He questioned my authority. He questioned my *allegiance*. I think of the officers out on West Florissant who turned their backs on me. Again I hear comments that now puncture the air behind me. I hear the word. This time I'm sure of it. It reverberates. It slices me.

I realize I have an opportunity to change all that. I can make things right. I can regain the officers' trust, renew their confidence in me. I can make a statement as a leader: *I am not just* with *you; I am* one *of you.*

I can gain their approval.

I want that—I admit it.

I want their trust.

I make a decision.

I decide to go.

☆

I locate the SWAT leader.

"Can you go down there and take back that store?" I ask him.

He looks at me, and I detect the trace of a smile.

I can read the answer in his face: *This is more like it.*

"Can you stop what's going on?" I ask him, doubling down on my decision, perhaps wanting extra reassurance, searching for any doubt or reservation.

"Yes," he says. "Absolutely."

"Well, have all the SWAT guys gear up."

A swirl of movement. The clack of equipment. The rustle of

gear snapping on. A hum of excitement. I feel a shift. A sudden wave of respect and relief rolls toward me. I hear no more negative comments. This moment—this decision—has elevated me.

I make eye contact with the SWAT leader. He nods. We're ready to go.

And then something happens.

The earth shakes beneath my feet.

My body—my entire being—trembles.

My ego, so pumped up a moment ago, deflates like a popped balloon.

I suddenly feel completely *selfish*.

It hits me. Hard. I have become so focused on how these police officers see me, how they feel about me, that I have allowed my pride to sway my leadership, to overwhelm my thinking.

Yes, I want their approval. But I have to lead from my heart.

I turn to the group gearing up closest to me and see two young female officers. I look into their eyes. I study their faces. I focus on one, her features obscured by the night shadows. I know it seems impossible, but her face becomes my daughter's face. As I look at this officer geared up and ready to go, I see my daughter looking back at me.

Then I look down the street at the young men hauling merchandise out of the smashed store windows, and I see boys . . . young *boys* . . . and I picture my own son.

Standing at the crest of the hill, I ask myself, *Am I willing to send these young men and women into a fight—into a battle—that may cost them their lives? Would I send my daughter down there? Should I send my fellow police officers down there to shoot my son?*

Please, God, don't let there be blood on my hands.

These thoughts are a blip, flashing through my mind in less than a second.

And in that span of time, I change my mind.

I won't do it. I won't send these troops down there.

"Stand down!" I say.

I rush over to the SWAT leader. "Tell everyone to stand down. We're not going."

He blinks in confusion.

"We're not going down there," I say emphatically, making sure he comprehends my words.

I don't know if I'm right, but I'm sure.

That's not true.

I *know* I'm right.

The police officers behind me lose it.

I hear the violence of their comments snarling at my back.

Distrust. Disbelief. Hatred. Thundering at me now.

I don't dare turn around.

Images flood my mind: A clenched fist. Fiery, furious eyes.

I hear the sound of men crying—actually crying—in anger.

And I hear words hurled like knives:

Traitor.

Coward.

Gutless.

You're with them.

And then . . . again . . . the word.

Two hundred-plus SWAT and police officers geared up for confrontation stand at the crest of the hill and watch a band of looters ransack the stores of Ferguson.

I stand in front of this assembled army and stare down the

street. I hear the words. I see the images—behind me, directed at me. I keep looking forward. I don't look back.

But I keep picturing my daughter and my son, and I say to myself, "I don't have the right."

And then I whisper, the words ringing in my head, "I don't have the *right*."

✯

Around two o'clock in the morning, after the streets have cleared, I return to the command post. Muscling my way through the chaos and anger that still envelop me, I walk into the bathroom, lock the door behind me, and slowly make my way over to the sink.

My chest heaves. My shoulders sag. I grip the corners of the sink to keep myself from collapsing. With a sigh, I raise my head and force myself to look in the mirror. My reflection howls. I look into my eyes—my bloodshot and tortured eyes—and I start to cry. I lower my head and stare into the sink as my sobs overtake me.

"God," I say. "This hurts so bad."

I choke down a sob, wipe my nose with my sleeve, and say, "I know I'm strong enough, I know I am, but it . . . hurts . . . so . . . *bad*."

I bow my head and say, "God, I feel so alone."

And then—very distinctly—I feel my head lifting. I open my eyes and look at myself in the mirror again.

I see a man.

I see a black man.

I see a father. A son.

"They don't see me," I say. "Nobody sees me."

I realize I'm feeling the same way the protesters feel.

Nobody sees them.

They might as well be invisible.

But I see them.

I see them because I *am* them.

We share the same heart, the same soul, the same pain.

"I am you," I hear myself say.

Then my heart turns to prayer.

"Thank you, God, for taking me through this turmoil. Thank you for allowing me to see—to see these hurting people and to see what they see. But it hurts. Change hurts. Change hurts so bad."

And then I whisper, "Please, God, let me be seen."

I have been to church many times in my life, and I have said many prayers, but I believe this is the first time I have ever truly prayed.

Standing in this bathroom, staring at my smudged reflection in the mirror, my shoulders shaking . . . sobbing over the sink, tears streaming down my face—yes, this is the first time I have ever really *prayed.*

DAY 8

SATURDAY, AUGUST 16, 2014

"NO MORE THAN I CAN BEAR"

"You were saved for something," she says.
"Don't die before you find out what.
What's your dream for your life?"

MARY KARR
LIT

I KEEP ASKING MYSELF THIS QUESTION:
What is a man?

In the early hours of Saturday morning, I exit the bathroom, walk slowly through the command post, and head out to the parking lot. I pass officers who won't look at me and others who turn their backs and mumble things I can't hear—things I don't want to hear. I step outside, and the night is warm and still. As I get into my car, my thoughts are scrambled, thrashing around in my mind.

What will I face tomorrow?
Will these guys support me?
Will they rally behind me?

Or will they say they've lost confidence in me and refuse to follow?

The streets of Ferguson are deserted and calm; the smell of smoke and fear are faint and fading.

I wonder, *When the sun rises, will I still be in command of my troops?*

My own faith has been strengthened. But I fear I have lost theirs.

⭐

At home, I can't sleep. I replay the moments of the day, and my emotions rise into my throat. I think about all the times when Lori, the kids, and I have talked about the consequences of being a cop.

The pressure.

The unknown.

The danger.

I have told them that the ultimate sacrifice for our family would always come from me. The weight would fall on me. As the man of the family, I would take on that responsibility. I vowed to make our family safe, but if anyone had to take the ultimate final fall, it would never be them. It would always, *always*, be me.

I saw tonight that it could happen in Ferguson.

I determined that if someone had to make the ultimate sacrifice, it would not be members of SWAT or officers assigned to quell the unrest on West Florissant. It would be me.

I think about death. I think about dying.

I decide to write a letter to Lori.

I envision a blank sheet of paper and begin to compose a farewell letter in my mind.

Dear Lori,

I love you.

I know that what has happened to me hasn't been fair, especially to you. I may not have been fair to you. But this was on me. This task—Ferguson—was on me. I knew I had to give whatever it took to stop the violence on the street. I wanted to walk with the people. I wanted to walk in my uniform, without wearing a vest. I'm sorry if that was careless. Lori, I'm sorry. I loved every minute of our life together, and I deeply love you.

I think about where I should leave the letter.

I know that Lori would not want to live in our house without me, so I decide to slip the letter underneath the mattress, on my side of the bed. I want to leave it in the place where I wept every night during the unrest in Ferguson. I picture her finding the letter the day she moves out of the house.

"Lori, please understand," I whisper, "if anyone must die, it has to be me."

★

Lying in bed, I see myself back on the crest of the hill, facing the police officers massed behind me. I shout, "Stand down!" and the police officers fade away and disappear. I'm left standing on the hill alone.

I roll off the bed and go into the bathroom. I close my eyes to douse my tears, and again I pray.

"God, tell me—did I do the right thing?"

Then I lose it and I wail, "What else could I have done?"

I don't remember returning to bed. I only remember drifting off to sleep to Lori's gentle breathing.

★

When I wake up on Saturday morning, one week after Michael Brown's death, I feel as if a weight has been lifted off my chest. I feel strangely . . . free. In spite of how everyone around me reacted, I know that I did the right thing last night.

I schedule an early news conference to start at eleven o'clock. I shower, dress, say good-bye to Lori, and go out to my car. But this morning, I don't go directly to Ferguson. I decide to stop at the cemetery where my father and brother are buried. I need to talk to my man team.

With the morning already warm and humid and sweat beading on my forehead, I face the oversize headstone—with my father's dates on the left, my brother's in the middle, and room for my mother's on the right. I feel myself swaying slightly. I close my eyes and picture my dad—towering over me, playing catch with me, sitting like a king in his armchair recliner in the living room. When I visit him here, I picture him before the accident—six foot two, ramrod straight, full Afro, stylish clothes, cool demeanor, a magnetic presence. He was a force, my dad; the powerful engine that drove our family.

I think about my brother now, gone way too young. Bernard, the life of every party, the center of every gathering, the de facto mayor of everywhere he went. He knew everybody and everybody knew him. So many people called him their best friend. I did too.

"I need you guys," I say. "I need my man team."

I sigh, fold my hands, and lower my head.

"Please surround me with your strength. I need your strength."

I open my eyes and look at my dad's inscription.

"Please, Dad, walk with me."

What is a man?

My dad.

☆

When I was twenty-seven years old, I started my third year as a trooper, and I began to lose my hair. At first, it thinned out on top, and then the *thinning* became *disappearing* as the area widened and formed into a small but prominent bald spot. Every morning, I spent way too much time working on my hair, getting it just right. It was a waste of time, because my hat immediately messed it all up. So even though I was required to wear my hat, I rarely did—unless my bosses came around.

At the same time, I started to feel as if I were being passed over for promotion. I compared myself to those troopers who were getting promoted, and frankly I was stumped. So I set up a meeting with Captain Bill Siebert, who was both a mentor and a friend.

When I closed the door to his office and told him I wanted to know where I stood, he picked up a sheet of paper that contained the names of all the troopers. Stabbing at the list of names with his fingernail, he moved his finger down the page . . . all the way to the bottom.

For a moment, I couldn't speak. I wanted to say, "Bill, I thought we were friends. How can you put me at the bottom of the list?"

Instead, I said nothing.

"Anything else I can do for you?" Bill asked.

"No. Thanks."

He had sent me a clear message: *Friendship doesn't mean*

favoritism. In his eyes, I hadn't yet earned a promotion. As I left Bill's office, I realized I had to change. I had to make a commitment to my career, take nothing for granted, and work to become the best trooper I could be.

Clearly you're not doing the things you need to do, I told myself.

I paused for a moment and then asked myself honestly, *Okay, what specifically am I not doing?*

For starters, Ron, you're not wearing your hat.

That night, after work, I shaved my head.

The next morning, I put on my hat. I wore it all through the day as a symbol of my new stance, my new attitude, my new confidence. I challenged myself to finish each day knowing I had given every ounce of myself at work, that I had been the very best Ron Johnson, state trooper, that I could be. The following year, when the next promotional test for corporal came up, I scored the highest grade in our troop.

As a corporal, in addition to my regular duties as a trooper, I joined SWAT. I didn't mind the time I spent patrolling alone in my car, but I loved being part of a team. Always have. And I admit that I craved the adrenaline rush that went along with being on SWAT.

I also discovered something else. I seemed to have a knack for being able to slow things down, to see the whole picture—at times, to see a completely different picture—even while feeling the adrenaline pumping. Some guys on SWAT would say that once they're in motion, their vision blurs. The opposite occurred with me. Everything to me appeared in slow motion. My vision heightened. I saw details. I saw depth. Perspective. I saw a person's past. A person's life.

One day, we burst into a vacated house, and I saw a few broken toys scattered on the floor and children's snacks left on the table. Even though there were no kids in the room, I could see them. I knew who they were. I could picture their poverty. I could see their parents—or single parent—struggling. I could feel the pain in their lives. We had been called in to deal with a domestic violence situation, but I saw beyond that.

I don't know how or why my mind works this way. I have a different kind of vision. My imagination fills in the blanks. I don't judge. I simply allow myself to *see*. And this reveals a different picture. I see . . . the humanity.

☆

What is a man?

It's not about putting on that uniform.

It's not about winning.

It's not about being a hero.

It's about *not* being a hero.

☆

I have never fired my gun in the line of duty.

I came close only once.

One day when I got called to an accident, I pulled over next to a wreck on the highway, a car tipped over on its side. As I approached the car, a large and very distraught man extracted himself from the mangled vehicle and suddenly charged toward me. He was red faced, jacked up, and he clearly wanted a piece of me.

I told him to please step back.

He kept coming.

I drew my weapon.

"Hey, hey, listen," I said. "I'm here to help you."

He kept coming. As he got closer, I could see the fear in his eyes. I think he must have seen the fear in my eyes, too, because he abruptly stopped. Within seconds, several firefighters and police officers surrounded him and subdued him, and then I handcuffed him.

Once he was secured, I returned to my car. I leaned against the hood as my stomach clenched, knotted up, and nausea rose in my throat.

I pictured myself several years earlier, sitting across the desk from a highway patrol officer during my initial interview to become a trooper.

"Can you take a life?" the trooper asked me.

"Yes," I replied, not hesitating at all. "Yes, I can."

I truly believed it then, but the trooper had asked me a hypothetical question. I had no true point of reference. The circumstance didn't exist, had never existed. It wasn't real to me.

But that experience on the side of the road—drawing my gun on an actual human being and only a moment away from pulling the trigger and taking his life—was all too real.

If you asked me that same question today, I don't know if I could say yes.

☆

I've had one fight.

I was arresting a drunk driver, and as he came weaving out of his car, he started throwing punches. I had no choice but to defend myself. I nailed him a couple of times, and he dropped to his knees. An ambulance came and took him to the hospital.

Later that night, I visited him. When he looked up from his hospital bed and recognized me, he looked distraught.

"I'm sorry I made you fight me," he said. "It was my fault. You don't have to write a report. You weren't to blame at all."

"No, I'm going to write a report," I said. But as I left the room, I thought, *What did I do wrong? How could I have avoided that?*

I still don't see how I could have responded any differently, but I think I felt worse than he did. I knocked that man down, but I didn't win the fight. I lost by having it.

☆

And I once arrested someone who simply refused to let me arrest him.

I stopped a guy for speeding and driving recklessly and asked him to get out of his car. When he did, I had to retreat several steps. The guy was huge. A former lineman at the University of Oklahoma, he went about six foot six and weighed well over three hundred pounds. His arms were so muscular and massive that he couldn't reach them behind his back to be handcuffed. I hoped he wouldn't throw a punch at me, because I knew I couldn't take him. When I told him he was under arrest, he glared at me and widened his stance.

"No, I'm not," he said.

"Yes, you are," I replied. "You need to turn around."

"I won't," he said. "You're not gonna arrest me."

In my mind, I quickly flipped through my options. I didn't come up with many.

"I guess if you're saying you're not under arrest, you're telling me you're free to go," I said.

He scrunched his forehead a little as he thought it over.

"If you do that," I said, "if you leave here, I wouldn't go to sleep if I were you. Because the next time you see me, there's gonna be a whole *lot* of me—and we are gonna arrest you."

He frowned again, his forehead creasing like an accordion.

"It's your choice," I said. "You can come now, or we'll find you later."

He grunted and then made his decision.

"Okay," he said, holding his wrists toward me.

★

What is the goal of every law enforcement officer?

It took me years, but I finally figured it out.

Every day needs to end the same way.

Nobody is big enough to win every battle. And some battles are not worth fighting. The situation dictates the outcome. But every outcome—every day—must end with the officer going home.

What is the goal of every man?

Each and every day, it's the same goal.

Three words.

To go home.

★

I rose quickly through the ranks.

Two years after becoming a corporal, I made sergeant. In my opinion, sergeant is the best rank of all. Becoming a sergeant brings with it a certain prestige. I felt like both a player and a coach. I now had responsibility for a *team*. I led an entire unit, seven troopers in all. I created traffic plans and made field decisions while still working the road *and* SWAT.

Then, only two years after becoming a sergeant, I made

lieutenant and was transferred to Kansas City. I moved out of the field into an office. Sergeants reported to me. I no longer worked SWAT. As foreign as the term sounded to me, I became "the establishment."

I experienced culture shock. I missed being among the guys and on the road every day. I missed the camaraderie. I missed the adrenaline rush of working SWAT.

One day, with two guys from SWAT on vacation, I got a call asking whether I'd be willing to fill in. I couldn't wait. But being a lieutenant, I was treated differently. When I started to go inside the house with the rest of the team, one of the guys stopped me and told me I had to stay outside.

"You're *administration*," he said.

I knew what that really meant. Although I had worked SWAT for years, I was now just a substitute—and *establishment* to boot. I waited outside as the other members of the team rushed inside the house.

"This feels so weird," I said to the air.

I hadn't realized how much I missed the action, the excitement. I wondered whether I had given up too much, whether I had moved up the ranks too quickly. Once again I asked myself the question that I seemed to face constantly: *Have I done the right thing?*

Eventually, I settled in to Kansas City, adjusted to my role as lieutenant, and even thrived. In Kansas City, I made perhaps my best friend in law enforcement: Jim Ripley. He helped me keep my sanity, even though together we were pretty much insane, always pulling pranks on each other.

One day, three years after I arrived in Kansas City, I heard that a captain's slot had opened up in St. Louis. Not only was it back home, but it was also the next rung up the ladder. I talked to Lori about the possibility of applying.

"I know we've only been here a few years," I said, "and it might be tough on the kids to move again; but if I don't apply for captain now, it could be a long time before I have another chance."

Lori didn't flinch, didn't hesitate. "Go ahead and try."

I knew it was a long shot because thirteen other people were applying for the position. On top of that, at thirty-eight years of age, I was extremely young to be considered for captain. I had only fifteen years on the force, far less time than anyone else in the running. The guys I was competing against all had at least eighteen years of experience, and many were already in their fifties.

Somehow, I made it over every hurdle. Finally, it came down to one last step: an interview with the colonel in charge and six of his staff members—five majors and one lieutenant colonel.

A few days before my interview, I called my buddy Jim Ripley. He always had his ear to the ground, and I wanted to know what he'd been hearing.

"Not much," he said. "People are mainly wondering if you're too young or if you have enough time on."

I had been thinking about the sorts of questions I might be asked—*What kind of leader will you be?*—and rehearsing my answers. Having gotten this far, I didn't think that my age or lack of experience would be serious obstacles. It seemed they would have already factored that in. Still, I couldn't dismiss Ripley's intel. I filed the information away and kept on preparing what I might say.

On the day of my interview, I thought about Grandfather Sherman, my dad's dad. When I was growing up, he lived on a small farm in Arkansas, and we visited him often. Something about him drew me. From as early as I can remember, we had a special bond. I spent as much time with him as I could, sometimes working beside him, picking peas. He was a humble man—quiet, proud, and wise. He treated everybody with respect, even the white people I observed who didn't treat him with respect.

Grandfather Sherman always held me accountable, asking how I was behaving in school, urging me to work hard. When I got older, we exchanged letters, and he always asked me if I was behaving. More than anything, I wanted him to attend my high school graduation, but he passed away shortly before the end of my senior year.

One day when we were picking peas, he said, "You're gonna become something, son. I got this feeling. You are gonna become something."

I always felt as if Grandfather Sherman were looking over my shoulder, keeping tabs on me. In a way, I feel he still does.

When I sat down for my captain's interview before a panel of seven staff members, the colonel in charge asked me a couple of preliminary questions, and then one of the majors asked me Jim Ripley's exact question.

"Why should we pick you?" he asked. "You've got only fifteen years on the force."

It hit me again.

Bias.

In this case, age bias.

Because I had already thought through the age issue, I was ready to respond. I had to believe that the colonel would recognize the bias, confront it, and hear me out.

I paused for a count of one . . . two . . . three . . . and then I said, "Sir, I would ask that you not judge me on what my age says I should be, but on what my actions say that I am."

"Wow," someone on the panel blurted out.

At that moment, I knew they would choose me.

I found out officially a few hours later, after I arrived home in Kansas City. Lori and I began to make plans to move back to St. Louis, where I would take on the responsibilities of a captain in the Missouri State Highway Patrol.

At the cemetery, just outside Ferguson, I stand facing my family's headstone and slowly bow my head. The quiet consumes me, soothes me. I sense the power of these departed souls—my father, my brother—and I feel at peace. A tiny smile lights my face. Eight days into the turmoil in Ferguson, a cemetery has become a place of comfort, just as a bathroom had become my sanctuary.

My father passed away from complications of Alzheimer's disease. Months after my mom moved him into a nursing home, the disease progressed and he needed to go to the hospital. For days, our family gathered in his hospital room, settling around him. We watched basketball, recalled family stories, remembered the good times, and laughed. How we laughed. There was no sense that this was a deathwatch. The time we spent during my dad's last days felt upbeat, almost like a warm family get-together. My father appeared completely present and engaged, taking everything in and enjoying—really enjoying—our company. Then, one afternoon, he died of a heart attack.

After the accident in San Francisco, my dad had learned to live with *less than*—less than the full ability to walk, less than the ability to play sports with his kids. After the Alzheimer's took hold, he had to learn how to live with less than the full ability to function mentally.

Here at the cemetery, looking at his gravestone, I see him the way he was when I was a child, when he was a police officer, when he was the father who played catch with me, when he was *that* man.

Now that he has passed on into eternity, I believe he is once again whole.

☆

I look at my brother's name on the headstone.

Bernard.

I relive the morning of his fatal motorcycle accident. The pain of that day—the physical *pain*—returns and grips my heart.

I didn't see the crash, but I can envision it. I have worked enough motorcycle accidents to recreate the scene in my mind—especially the aftermath: the stillness, the sorrow.

Nobody knows exactly what happened, but I do know that Bernard was on his bike in the early morning and veered off the road at high speed. And I know he hit something and was killed instantly.

That morning, a Sunday, my dad called to tell us. He was in the early stages of Alzheimer's, and for a moment I thought he had made it up or dreamed Bernard's accident. But after he broke down in tears, I knew he was telling the truth.

For months afterward, I was in a numbing state of shock. The grief would hit me in waves, and so many thoughts bored into my brain, along with the inevitable *Why?* Along with that searing question came the haunting sadness that I never got to say good-bye.

I tried to lose myself in my work, in gospel music, in sitting by myself and remembering the times we'd had together, in weeping, in spending time with friends and family who knew him and loved him.

Distracting myself didn't help. Prayer didn't help. Nothing helped. I couldn't find anything to take away the pain.

One night, I spoke with one of my neighbors, who's a pastor. He, of course, knew about my brother and asked how I was doing. I told him that I still felt enormous pain. I asked him, "How long is it going to take for me to get over this?"

My neighbor looked at me and said, "Ron, you'll never 'get over it,' so don't even try."

I needed to accept the grief.

Allow the pain.

Realize that I would never get over the pain of my brother's death.

I needed to hear that and acknowledge it.

That knowledge gave me strength.

And the pastor was right.

I've never gotten over it.

☆

Seeing that it's time to get on to work, I whisper thanks to my father and my brother, and I start walking back to my car.

Though nothing will ever take away the pain, accepting the grief and allowing the pain have shown me this: I am strong enough. I can stand.

✮

Eleven a.m. We hold the press conference in a local church building, and the meeting room is packed with local and national press and people who've spent their days and nights walking the streets of Ferguson protesting, making their voices heard.

Before Governor Nixon approaches the podium, he whispers to me, "Ron, you did the right thing last night. Don't think twice about it."

"Thank you," I mumble as the governor moves to the podium.

He begins by thanking and praising law enforcement. He rushes through a few other sentences to get to the purpose of his appearance today: He is imposing a curfew from midnight until five o'clock tomorrow morning. The crowd in the auditorium roars in disapproval. Many of their words are indecipherable to me, but their emotions are clear: surprise, anger, outrage.

The governor hastily folds his sheet of paper and nods at me. I take his place at the podium.

"The governor has enacted a curfew to allow us to provide safety for the citizens of Ferguson, but also to maintain the right of the people," I say, competing with the crowd to be heard. "We will enforce that curfew in an effort to provide safety and security to the area."

I pause several seconds for the crowd to quiet down before I continue.

"We won't enforce it with trucks. We won't enforce it with tear gas. We will communicate. We will talk to you when it's time to go home."

More shouting erupts, the anger now coming hard. I wave my hand, waiting for the shouts to subside.

"Last night's events precipitated that response," I say. "You saw that. You *saw* that. But I can tell you that tonight, if someone is standing in the street, an armored truck is not going to come out. You saw people sitting in the street. You saw that, too. They will have a chance to get up. And that's the way it's going to continue."

Sudden applause drowns me out. Stunned, I step back from the podium as the applause builds and fades and people start screaming questions at me. I swivel from one side of the room to the other, trying to hear what people are asking.

"One question at a time," I say.

A broadcaster's deep voice booms, trampling every other sound in the room. "Were you not aware—even though you are in command—that SWAT teams were being deployed last night?"

"Yes," I say. "I was aware."

"You gave that order?"

"Yes."

"And you ordered the tear gas?"

"No."

The crowd reacts, roars. The guy with the broadcaster's voice shouts something I can't make out about the use of tear gas. I want to respond to him, but he goes off shouting about something else I can't hear, and then other people scream questions over his. I shake my head and peer in the direction of that booming voice.

"Can I answer the question?" I say.

More shouts, and then someone yells, "Let him answer the question."

The uproar slowly fades and the room goes quiet. The man with the booming voice takes the floor, shushing the crowd. He speaks calmly but pointedly.

"There are reports that this happened without your knowing it."

Amazing, I think. *Everyone knows everything and hears everything. Every rumor is scrutinized and analyzed.*

Policing in a fishbowl—that's what this feels like.

Maybe that's what we need.

I take a breath and count: One . . . two . . . three . . .

"Last night we had several officers who were trapped in a parking lot," I say. "They tried to get out. We sent two armored vehicles to help them out. An officer deployed one can of tear gas. *One.* He was there. He made that decision. I got a call at home and said, 'I am back en route.' I got out of my bed and I went back. I said to the officer, 'Make sure we don't use any more tear gas. Do not use any that is not necessary.' That is what I said."

A rush of questions rise, overlap, and veer off into muddled shouts. I pick up only scattered words: "rubber bullets," "tear gas," "Darren Wilson," "curfew," "tear gas," "tear gas," "*tear gas . . .*"

Overwhelmed, I step to the side. Someone takes my place at the podium and indicates that the news conference has come to an end. With an uproar at my back, I join a scrum of officers heading out the door toward cars that will take us to the command post. As soon as we step outside, the officers begin to attack me with their questions, their accusations.

"Why did you tell them you weren't going to deploy tear gas?" one of the commanders asks.

"I didn't say that."

"Yes, you did."

I know what I said: *I wouldn't enforce the curfew with tear gas.*

My intention felt clear to me. If protesters or looters don't comply with the curfew, or if they break the law, I will do what I have to do.

"You said you were not deploying tear gas," the commander insists.

I sigh, the weight of this moment crushing me.

"That's not what I said."

I take another breath, and then I explain.

"If the behavior is correct and nobody is causing any issues, I will not be using tear gas. I thought that was clear. I think everyone got that."

"You know, Ron, I'm supporting you," the commander says, his eyes aflame. "But you're making it hard."[1]

☆

I cruise Ferguson with CNN's Don Lemon, who interviews me as we ride through town. Don talks about doing a special hour devoted to Ferguson, focusing on how the community responds to the police. I think that story should be told. Still, I feel guarded, uncomfortable. I focus my attention on doing my job, trying to forget about the microphone wired to my shirt and the camera shadowing my every move.

This, too, is part of the job, I tell myself.

☆

I walk along West Florissant past the concrete slab of the former QuikTrip. Don Lemon trails me, just out of camera range. At my suggestion, the city has erected a chain-link fence around the site to prevent looters from congregating here and claiming this spot as some kind of shrine or testament to violence. As I walk by on the sidewalk, an elderly woman in a splashy pink pantsuit, carrying a matching pink umbrella to protect herself from the brutal rays of the midday sun, approaches me. We talk briefly and she smiles warmly, almost lovingly. As she continues on her way, she stops for a moment and turns back.

"I just wanted to come over and holler at you," she says.

"Well, I'm glad you did. Feels good just to be able to walk out here and relax and be in the neighborhood, doesn't it?"

"It feels safe," she says. "I've been living in this neighborhood forever, and this is the first time I've ever felt this safe."

"A new day is coming," I say, surprised at how passionate I sound.

Don and I continue to walk. He asks me a few questions along the way, but mostly we just observe. We come to a row of burned-out and boarded-up storefronts on West Florissant. Outside, on a short concrete wall, a group of young men and a couple of young women in their late teens or early twenties sit and look off, trying to appear nonchalant, cool, and disinterested. As Don and I and the cameraman approach, I say hello and shake their hands. Don smiles, puts his hands on his hips, and says to the group, "How you doing?"

One of the young men says to me, "Can I get my picture taken with you?"

"Sure."

"So," Don says, the bright sun causing him to squint, "the police don't really get out and mingle with you guys, do they?"

"No, they don't," a young man in a tank top replies in a muted, nearly inaudible voice.

The guy next to him, wearing a T-shirt and a baseball cap turned backward and tilted, says in a bold voice, "The only time they come out here is when they lock us up or something. Let me tell you like this . . ."

He cocks his head at the kid in the tank top.

"Me and him are standing in front of my house about a month ago. I see a police car go past, up the street. I knew he was gonna come back. He came back about two minutes later. He said—"

"'Was we smoking marijuana—'" Tank Top jumps into the conversation.

"'—over at some apartment complex?'" Baseball Cap says. "I was like, 'No, we just stepped outside my house.' We were *three blocks away* from where he was talking about."

Don Lemon nods and says, "You don't feel that police officer is part of the community . . ."

"No, I don't," Tank Top replies.

"Not at all," Baseball Cap chimes in. "All they want to do is take us in. Get us off the streets."

A young man I haven't seen before—shirtless, wearing a long, bushy goatee—says, "The thing is, you all probably heard this from Mom or Grandma or somebody: How you approach somebody is how they'll approach you back."

I nod in recognition of the truth. "There you go," I say.

The shirtless young man says, "How you come to somebody is what make us go, 'Hold on, why you coming at me like that? Why you grabbing on me? Can you explain to me what I did? What was the reason you're messing with me in the first place?' If I'm on the sidewalk, he could've said, 'You're on the sidewalk.' Whatever the reason is, he could've got out of his car and approached me like a *man* instead of cursing. Why couldn't he be, 'Listen, young man, let me talk to you for a second.' I might stop and listen to what you got to say. But if you jump out at me with animosity and stuff like that? I'm gonna make you do your job today."

Don Lemon takes this in. "So if an officer approaches you with respect, you will respond with respect."

"Yeah," says the shirtless young man. "They're approaching us like we already committed a violent crime. Or like you caught me selling dope or something. You pulled me over, why? Because my pants were sagging?"

The shirtless young man stands up to demonstrate.

"If he says, 'Could you pull them up?' I say, 'I can pull them up, officer, no problem' instead of 'Pull them up! PULL THEM UP!'"

The shirtless young man sits back down on the low concrete wall. He looks me in the eye. I see frustration. I see resignation.

Nothing's gonna change.

He doesn't speak the words, but I see it in his face.

He shakes his head, sadly. When he speaks now I hear pain.

"Man, look," he says.

Look.

See me.

Look.

That is what so many young people of color feel.

To the police, they are either committing a crime . . . or they're invisible.

Strangely, the exchange with these young men fills me with hope. When we get back in the car, with the camera rolling, Don leans over the backseat and says, "That was good. I think they heard you. One guy even took his picture with you."

I stare out the window.

"This is what we should have been doing all along," I say.

☆

As the afternoon heats up, I walk. The sweat pours through me. My shirt sticks to my skin. I feel raw and grimy. A woman runs out of the crowd and hands me a bottle of water. I thank her and slug it down. I keep walking. I shake hands with countless people. I hug some. Several people call my name. Several more clap for me. At one point, a man walks alongside me for several minutes.

"All this here," he says, "feels like a fraternity."

He says he felt the same way in college when he joined Kappa Alpha Psi, a black fraternity, one of nine historic black fraternities and sororities known as the Divine Nine.

"I was in Kappa Alpha Psi," I say, laughing.

We stop on the street and pose, flashing the Kappa Alpha Psi hand signals, sharing a goofy, incongruous moment in the middle of a protest march. The CNN camera records us. People snap our picture with their phones. People immediately post the pictures on Twitter, Facebook, and Instagram. The posts go viral.

An hour later, I'm buried by a storm of hatred.

"Captain Johnson posed with a protester, flashing gang signs."

That's what they're saying.

What's worse is what I hear from several police officers.

"I knew it," a cop mutters as I walk by.

I hear worse. Much worse.

"Oh, I really want to do a special about this," Don Lemon says as we drive.

"No," I say. "Don't make a big deal about it. Let it fade away."

I say that, but I don't believe it will.

☆

The Saturday swelter burns into evening. My legs feel like lead. My back aches. Today I feel as if everything has piled on, one thing after another—the curfew, the news conference, the fraternity signs mistaken for gang signs. The NAACP and other groups rail against the curfew, calling it unfair and discriminatory. Several officers keep a running, nasty dialogue with me about not planning to deploy tear gas. Other officers don't want to deal with me at all and simply walk away. And even though I explain repeatedly that I flashed fraternity signs and not gang signs, and several other people, including newscasters, confirm this, I continue to receive icy, hateful stares from officers in my own command.

Midnight approaches. The large crowd that had congested the street begins to thin out.

I hear people saying as they leave, "Hey, we've got to go home. Mom said we have to go home."

I watch the streets clear and hear a different tone, something more cooperative and conciliatory, and I think almost in disbelief, *The curfew is working.*

I'm not only premature; I'm also wrong.

☆

I go back to the command post. I find a desk and start jotting down notes for a late-night news conference. Suddenly I hear shouting from outside—a commotion, building to a melee—and somebody shouts, "They're coming!"

I step outside and see a massive crowd—at least twice the size of the earlier crowd—gathered on the street. Unlike the evening's peaceful protesters, this group is on a mission of violence, fueled by rage.

They begin to rush toward the command post, throwing bricks, rocks, bottles. Several people in the crowd light Molotov cocktails. I hear gunshots coming from several different directions.

We take cover.

My heart pounding and a sense of sadness and defeat pulsing through me, I order SWAT to deploy—*with* tear gas. I feel I have no choice.

Armored vehicles roll out. Officers lob tear gas canisters into the crowd descending on the command post. Within moments, the tide of the battle turns. Make no mistake: That's what this is. A battle.

The crowd halts and retreats, with SWAT and other officers in pursuit. Shielded by the armored vehicles, they charge down the street—and come to an abrupt stop. The protesters have erected a series of barriers—stacks of bricks that resemble rough, jagged walls—forcing the police to stop and allowing the protesters to escape. The street becomes a deafening, discordant orchestra of screaming, coughing, gagging, gunfire, and the piercing blare of sirens. Gray clouds billow from smoke canisters, blinding and choking the protesters running along the street. People claw at their eyes from the tear gas.

Chaos.

The word lodges itself in my brain.

The images swim in front of my eyes.

I feel as if everything has gotten away from us—from me, from everyone. Two days ago, before I took charge of security in Ferguson, our community seemed stuck. And then a ray of hope, a sliver of light. Our community went from several consecutive nights of hell to one good, peaceful day. I saw promise. We had taken a step forward.

Now I feel staggered, as if we'd been sucker punched, that sliver of light snuffed out.

I hope the people I've walked with understand that I had to use tear gas. The rioters attacked us. We were completely vulnerable. I had to protect our police officers. I didn't make the decision lightly, but it was an easy decision to make.

My sense of time is distorted, as if in a dream, but finally the crowd disperses. The streets become eerily empty. The night shuts down and settles into an uneasy tranquility, as if nothing out of the ordinary had occurred. But the shards of glass, mounds of scattered and broken bricks, residue of smoke, and stench of tear gas betray that tranquility. These nights in Ferguson are as fraught, as frustrating, as frightening, as painful as any nights I have experienced—or will experience—in my lifetime.

My boots grinding through puddles of glass, I make my way back to the command post. I know that the media will be converging here shortly. I will speak to them, describe the events of the night, and try to hold back the aching in my heart.

☆

One-forty a.m.

I stifle the pain, to a degree, but I can't hold back my anger.

The media form a horseshoe around me, and the rage I feel floods out. I don't raise my voice. I don't have to.

I talk first about my disappointment—that we had to use tear gas; that an army of protesters . . . no, rioters . . . no, *criminals* . . . amassed on the street and charged the command post.

I explain how, for three days, I have walked among the people, telling everybody that we are in this together.

"We are partners in this," I say, my voice cracking.

"I support your rights," I say to the media assembled around me, and to everyone who will hear this. "I support your freedoms."

I pause.

"And I support these police officers."

I can't say what I'm feeling the most right now—that we had achieved some calm and taken a step forward, but that calm was destroyed—and now we only have chaos.

My heart sinks. I can't contain my disappointment.

I lower my head and I think about all the issues I talked about with people as we walked—a stew of concerns and justifiable complaints.

Crushing unemployment.

Low-wage jobs.

Poor schools.

Crippling poverty.

Crime.

Drugs.

Terrible relationships with the police.

All of it.

"Tonight," I say, my voice drifting off, waving away the impending onslaught of questions, "I feel so, so disappointed."

When the news conference ends, I go into the bathroom and break down.

Gripping the sink, staring up at the ceiling, tears running down my face, I wail, "Why am I all alone?"

I catch myself. I shake my head. I want to apologize.

"I'm sorry," I say. "I'm sorry for having these doubts—"

I slam my eyes shut. I squeeze hard enough for my eyelids to ache.

"It's been so tough. *So* tough. Thank you for giving me the strength to get through a day like today."

I pause. I can't explain how I know this, but I know we haven't come to the worst of it. I sense harder days ahead. Much harder.

I open my eyes and something fills me up. A rush of power. An infusion of energy—and hope—rockets through me like an electric charge. It feels like a spiritual jump start.

"I know you're not giving me more than I can bear," I say. "I know that."

I have to believe that, or else I have nothing.

DAY 9

SUNDAY, AUGUST 17, 2014

"I AM YOU"

Would you rather flood your heart or
dare let them see you cry?

BEN HARPER
"HOW DARK IS GONE"

I GET INTO BED around two-thirty in the morning, but sleep escapes me. After a few hours, I roll out of bed, shave, shower, dress, and join my family for breakfast. At the table, we don't say much, but afterward, as I'm preparing to head back to Ferguson, my daughter, Amanda, comes back into the kitchen. Through these days and long nights, I worry about what she and my son, Brad, must be hearing from friends, acquaintances, mainstream media, and indirectly from social media. I have asked her and Brad to stay off Facebook and Twitter until these days pass.

"How're you doing?" I ask.

"I'm okay." Amanda tilts her head. "You?"

"I'm all right."

She pauses for a second, then asks, "You scared?"

I exhale. "Yes."

She looks surprised at my answer.

"Not scared for me," I say. "For all of us. For our community. For our *country*."

I stop and think for a moment.

"I don't mean to sound so dramatic," I say. "But it's real. And it's—hard."

Amanda takes my hands. "You knew it would be."

"I did." I put my arms around her. "It's harder than I thought."

⭐

On my way to Ferguson, I stop for gas. As I flip open my gas tank, a woman at the next pump nods at me and says shyly, "I just want to tell you that we appreciate what you're doing."

"Thank you."

"We heard you last night on TV," she says. "We *all* feel disappointed. Just don't let it get you down."

"I won't."

My phone buzzes. I fish it out of my pocket and see a text from Amanda.

Remember, Daddy, when Peter failed, Jesus picked him back up.

I sniff and look over at the woman at the next pump.

"Today's another day," she says.

"Yes," I say, glancing back at Amanda's text. "A better day."

⭐

As scheduled, I meet three other officers at the command post. We plan to attend a combination rally and memorial service for Michael Brown at Greater Grace Church. I hear someone say that hundreds of people—perhaps as many as a thousand—will attend.

Members of Michael Brown's extended family have asked me to say a few words. I agreed, but to be honest, I haven't had a moment to think about what I'll say. What can I possibly say? I know I'll think of something. Even though I have nothing prepared, I don't feel pressure. I don't think about my speech at all. Something tells me not to worry. The words will come.

As we walk out to the car, my cell phone rings. On the display I see the name Bret Johnson—my superior, my boss, my friend.

"How you doing?" Bret says when I answer.

"I'm *doing*," I say.

"Well . . . ," he says. He pauses and sighs, and I can hear the struggle and discomfort in his voice. "You know, you've been working pretty hard. We can tell from the news conference last night that you're tired."

"We're all tired," I say.

"Last night, when you said you were disappointed in the governor's curfew—"

"I didn't say that."

"See, you're so tired you don't remember. That's what we mean. You're doing so much, you probably don't even recall what you said."

"I know what I said. I did say I was disappointed, yeah. I was talking to the citizens. I was disappointed in how last night turned out. I wasn't talking about anything else."

Bret starts to respond, but I jump in first.

"In fact, the people out here know what I meant. They said, 'We could tell we disappointed you last night.' And then they said, 'Don't let it get you down. Keep on going.' They understood."

"Well—" Bret sighs. I can picture him furrowing his forehead and rubbing his eyes.

"Well . . . ," he says for the third time, "from here on out, we're going to use the public information officers to talk to the media."

"You mean—"

I know exactly what he means, but I don't believe it.

"You won't be doing any more news conferences or press interviews," Bret says. "The public information people will be taking over."

I survey the faces of the three officers waiting for me. I need to erase all emotion from my face. I need to show them nothing. I need to bury the anger and disappointment I'm feeling.

"Okay," I say.

"Good," Bret says.

I want to argue. I want to defend myself. I want to shout at Bret. I want to scream at the world. I know he doesn't realize what he has done.

He has taken away my voice.

"Okay."

In the car on the way over to the church, I say nothing. One of the officers, picking up on how quiet I am, possibly even feeling the anger and hurt I have buried just beneath the surface, says, "You okay? You seem preoccupied."

"I am. Yes. I'm preoccupied."

When we arrive at the church, I see that the place is packed—every seat taken, people standing and leaning against the walls. I recognize members of the media, some crouching in front of the stage behind the TV cameras.

I make my way to the stage. Several people are scheduled to speak. I'm told that I will be called first.

As I take my place on the stage, I close my eyes and try to settle myself.

I've lost my voice.

The thought will not go away, but as I mull it over in my mind, the anger I've been feeling dissolves. It is replaced by a kind of sadness, followed by a sense of resolve.

I've lost my voice, I repeat silently to myself. In that regard, I'm like the people I've been walking with every day who feel that they *have* no voice.

But at least for today—at least for this moment—I will not be speechless.

I still have no idea what I'm going to say. I have nothing written down. I have formulated no particular thoughts. But if this is going to be my last public speech, I know that I must open myself up, go as deep as I can, and let the words flow.

God will take care of the rest, I think. *God will speak through me.*

I feel that.

I will allow God in.

I will speak from my soul.

★

As I step to the podium, I scan the faces of the people in front of me. Although it's a massive crowd, I try to look into the eyes of each person. I begin to speak, and it feels as if the words come not from my mind, not from my conscious thoughts, but from a source inside me. I have given myself up to something bigger than myself, as if I'm merely a vessel, a conduit through which these words must be spoken.

"Good evening," I hear myself say.

"Good evening," the crowd chants back.

I clasp my hands in front of me. I feel the softness of my

own skin. I make eye contact with members of Michael Brown's family, who are sitting in the front row.

"I want to start off by talking to Mike Brown's family."

The room goes silent.

"I want you to know that my heart goes out to you." I pause and keep my eyes fixed on them. "And I say that I'm sorry."

I point to my chest.

"I wear this uniform, and I should stand up here and say that I'm sorry."

I am not prepared for what happens next.

The people in the church begin to applaud. The applause builds—slowly at first, and then with more force. Gradually the applause rises into cheering, and everyone in the church stands, continuing to applaud and cheer. I hear the applause and the cheering, and I lose track of time. It seems to go on forever. Later I hear that the applause lasted for almost a full minute.

I wait for complete silence before I continue, and then I say, "This is *my* neighborhood. You are my family. You are my friends. And I am you."

More applause.

"And I will stand and protect you. I will protect your right to protest."

The crowd roars again. I feel my tears coming.

"I'm telling you right now," I say, trying not to cry, "I'm full right now—"

I bite my lip to hold back my tears.

"I came in here today, and I saw people cheering and people clapping—and *this* is what the media needs to put on TV."

The crowd again leaps up, applauding, cheering, roaring. I lower my head and close my eyes. When I open them again, the bluntness and honesty scorch my throat as I say, "The last twenty-four hours have been tough for me. I did an interview last night, and the reporter said, 'Something's wrong. Your tone has changed.' He said, 'Are you tired? Or is something bothering you?' And I said, 'My heart is heavy,' because last night I met some members of Michael Brown's family. . . . They brought tears to my eyes and shame to my heart. But I can tell you, and I've said it before, my daughter wrote me a thing in a text, and it talked about Peter and Jesus."

The crowd reacts, applauds, cheers.

"She said, 'Daddy, I know you're going to get scared.' I said, 'Yes, I am. Not scared for me, but scared for us.' And she said, 'Daddy, when Peter failed, Jesus picked him back up.'"

Over building applause, I say, "I needed today to get back in the water. I'm going to tell you I'm going to be here as long as it takes. My words will be honest. If we talk about it behind closed doors, I'm going to tell you. So if you don't want me to know, don't tell me behind closed doors."

I feel my voice rise.

"Because when *this* is over"—I unclasp my hands and point off with my left hand—"I'm gonna go in *my* son's room—*my* black son—who wears his pants sagging, wears his hat cocked to the side, got tattoos on his arms . . . but that's *my* baby."

The sheer emotion of the crowd lifts everybody to their feet—every single one. They stand in unison, clapping, screaming, and cheering. I wait but they don't stop applauding or shouting. I have to speak over them.

"And we all ought to be thanking the Browns for Michael. Because Michael's gonna make it better for our sons, so they can be better black men; so they can be better for our daughters, so they can be better black women; better for me, so I can be a better black father; and we know they're going to make our mamas even better than they are today."

I pause and nod.

"Let's continue to show this nation who we are. . . . But when these days are over and Mike Brown's family is still weeping, and they're still on their knees praying, no matter what *positive* comes in our lives, we still need to get on our knees, and we need to *pray*. We need to thank Mike for his life. We need to thank him for the change that is going to make us better."

I shake my head as the crowd roars.

"I love you," I say. "I stand tall with you." I point to the door of the church. "And I'll see you out there."[1]

★

I exit the stage, the roar of the crowd booming at my back. A minister I had spoken with earlier begins to hustle me toward the door and outside.

"I'm sorry to rush you," he says, "but the family doesn't want any police here."

"I understand."

"That was very moving, Captain Johnson," he says. "Do you think I could get a copy of it?"

"I don't have any copies," I say. "I just spoke spontaneously from my heart."

"Excuse me?"

Anthony Gray, a man I know well and the attorney for Michael Brown's mom and dad, stops the minister a moment before we reach the door. Anthony looks at me, clasps my hands, and nods. "The parents would like to see you," he says.

I leave the minister and follow Anthony down a hall and into a small room. Anthony closes the door behind me. Michael's parents are standing across the room. I slowly walk over to them. When I reach them, I see a blank, vacant look on their faces. Death masks. Looks beyond pain and sorrow. Looks beyond tears, beyond shock, beyond disbelief. Their eyes are filled with nothing but raw and naked sadness. Grief. Pure grief. I have seen grief like this only once before—in my parents' eyes after my brother died.

I step up to Michael Brown's parents and I say, simply, "I'm very sorry for your loss." And then very softly I say, "I'm sorry for the loss of your son."

They lift their eyes and look at me now, simultaneously, and I feel a kind of fire burning from their eyes into my heart. It's as if they were staring *into* me. I have never seen a look like that. Their eyes lacerate me—with pain, with anger, with loss, with accusation, and with deep, unanswerable questions.

Why did this happen?

How could this happen?

How could you let this happen?

How will I go on with my life?

How will I love?

How will I live?

In my mind, I hear the cry of that young man I spoke to with the bandanna masking his face.

We need answers.

I have no answers.

There are no answers.

I realize suddenly, certainly, without a doubt, without question, that *faith* is all we have.

With my head down and my legs heavy, as if I am sloshing through thick, murky water, I leave Michael Brown's parents and slowly exit the church. I find the three other officers waiting by the car. One sniffs and nods, acknowledging with a swipe of his cheek, the flicking away of a tear, that my words had moved him. Another officer looks past me, as if I weren't even there. The third officer glares at me. I read his look clearly: "You took their side. You are one of *them*."

☆

We get into the car, and almost immediately my cell phone rings. I glance at the display and once again see the name Bret Johnson.

I place the phone to my ear and say, "Hey."

"Hey."

After a long silent beat, Bret begins to speak, his voice thin and trembling.

"I just got a call from the governor's office about your speech at the church."

"Yeah?"

"You're going to continue giving press interviews and doing news conferences."

"What about our previous conversation?"

"Never happened."

I look at the three officers riding with me. They want to know what's going on, but I won't reveal to them the purpose of the call or the mix of emotions I feel—relief, validation, exoneration, maybe even . . . happiness.

"Okay," I say.

"Good," Bret says. "And Ron?"

"Yes?"

"This is the way it should be."

I feel a shift—an emotional, spiritual shift. My words at Greater Grace Church—impromptu, spontaneous, straight from my soul—are evidence of this shift. My world, as I know it, has changed.

I don't have to understand why or ask, *Why me?* Those questions don't matter. This isn't about me. All that matters is that I take charge and that I lead from my heart. I must commit to this. I can't lead by guessing what people want or by accommodating anybody. Though I have many decisions to make—some coming at me by the minute, if not by the second—leading from the heart means I must respond from goodness, and I have to be alive and aware in the moment. I know what's right. That knowledge is deep in my soul.

I believe this shift has come from God.

Though I have questioned him at various times in my life—have questioned his reasons, his *why*, I now know clearly, without a doubt, that whatever God intends to be revealed will be revealed. Or *not* revealed. It doesn't matter.

Just lead, I tell myself.

And communicate.

Leading is communicating.

As we drive back to the command post in Ferguson, it occurs to me: *I have my voice back.*

☆

Everyone at the command post has seen my speech on television. When I walk in, I get the same mixture of responses I received from the three officers I rode with. A few officers stare at me, their eyes hot with anger, but then they drift off and avoid me. Many officers come over to shake my hand. Several hug me.

Several have tears in their eyes. One officer thanks me for my honesty. Another says that now, for the first time, he believes I'm for the badge as well as for looking out for the people on the street. I can see that he now understands that I've been walking down the middle of that precarious road.

I go into my sanctuary—the bathroom—lock the door, grip the sink, and pray. I feel a change. A lightness. I no longer feel as if I'm carrying the burden of being in charge of security at Ferguson. Instead I feel that this charge is an honor. I might even call it a gift. I thank God for giving me this gift.

★

Back on the streets of Ferguson again, I walk. At first my legs feel weary. My back slumps, and my stride feels slow. But then more people join the group that's walking with me . . . and then even more. I pick up my pace, straighten my back, and walk with renewed purpose. I shake hands. People on the sidewalk wave, clap, and burst into the crowd just to hug me.

I walk for an hour . . . and then I walk for thirty more minutes. The heat and humidity, even hotter and thicker than yesterday, press down on me. At one point, as I stop to shake hands with several people, a woman reaches into a bag she's carrying and gives me a hand towel. I hesitate.

"It's fresh," she says, laughing. "I pulled it out of the wash this morning."

I smile, feeling a little embarrassed, but she seems not at all offended. Before I know it, she takes the towel back from my hand and begins to wipe the sweat off my face. As she dabs my forehead, she gently palms my cheek with her other hand—the same gesture a mother would use to dry off her baby's face.

"Keep it," the woman says, pressing the towel back into my hand.

"Thank you."

☆

My phone rings and I step aside to take the call. At first I can't make out what's being said on the other end. The line is full of static, and the voice is garbled. But then I hear, or I think I hear, "Please hold for Reverend Sharpton."

"Hello?" I say into the silence.

The static dissolves and I hear clearly, "Captain Johnson?"

"Yes."

"This is Al Sharpton."

I recognize the voice. I'd know it anywhere. I find myself grinning.

"Yes, hello, Reverend Sharpton."

"I know you're a busy man, but I just wanted to tell you that I've been watching you—everybody's watching you—and even if you feel down, or disappointed, just keep doing what you're doing."

"I will," I say.

"You're doing it right."

"Thank you."

Static.

Silence.

☆

I walk at dusk. I feel free. I no longer care how people view me. I no longer worry whether people judge me as a success or a failure. I turn all my focus to bringing about peace.

As I walk, I can tell that people are looking at me differently. Now even more people bring me towels to wipe off the sweat. More people bring me water bottles to quench my thirst. But most of all, more people want to talk.

Really talk.

I see myself now as the type of policeman I have always wanted to be.

I see myself as a father figure.

When I was a kid, I always thought of a policeman as another father, as a hero. As I walk now, I picture my dad, my hero. That's who I want to be: my dad. I want to fill those shoes. I want to wear the shoes I wore when we played "Family."

I feel my life has come full circle. Everything I have ever done—every experience I've ever had—has in some way prepared me for this moment. Being a crossing guard, deciding to become a trooper, the years I spent as a trooper, my time on SWAT, leading with empathy first, experiencing the pain of my father's and my brother's deaths—all of it—has gotten me ready. I am ready.

People say they will pray for me. I see some people praying for me now, forming a prayer circle, holding hands, their eyes closed, their bodies dipping and swaying. As I watch them, my tears begin to flow.

Some people come up to me and repeat words and phrases from my speech. I can barely remember what I said. The speech remains a blur, the words channeled from some reservoir within me, but people keep bringing me back to it. They shout, "This is *my* neighborhood, Captain Johnson" and "I stand tall with you" and, again and again, "*I am you.*"

I decide to dispatch teams of six or seven officers, white and black, to walk among the people. I send a few groups out now—late Sunday afternoon. At first the officers stand in a line and barely speak with the protesters. Then, gradually, I see the wall of resistance teeter and come down. The officers begin to have conversations with people. I see a few policemen and protesters laughing. I don't sense a real connection yet, but I see the effort—and I'll take it.

Inches, I tell myself. *This will happen slowly . . . by inches.*

But this will happen.

Then night falls.

☆

On Sunday night, we experience our worst night of clashes, of chaos. Violence explodes. Fires light up the night. Criminals come from outside Ferguson and infiltrate the protesters. They turn a peaceful assembly into a dangerous mob. Hell takes over the city and holds the streets for hours. Finally, our officers gain control.

At 1:25 a.m. Monday morning, I hold a press conference. I feel drained, upset, and bitterly disappointed. Worst of all, I see no end to the conflict. I jot down my observations and thoughts, and as I begin to read my statement, my hands are surprisingly steady even though my entire being trembles with anguish.

"Good morning. I want to start out by thanking the men and women of the Highway Patrol, St. Louis County, St. Louis City, and all the municipal police departments. They did a fine job tonight protecting the citizens of Ferguson. Tonight—"

Suddenly my head is pounding. I squint at what I have written, look up at the assembled members of the media, sigh, and continue with my prepared statement.

"Tonight—a Sunday that started with prayers and messages of unity, peace, and justice, took a very different turn after dark."

I pause, suddenly feeling incredibly, deeply sad.

"Molotov cocktails were thrown. There were shootings, looting, vandalism, and other acts of violence that clearly appear to not have been spontaneous, but premeditated criminal acts designed to damage property, hurt people, and provoke a response. This was not civil disobedience, but preplanned agitation and aggression."

I look up again from my notes and tell myself, *Stop reading. Speak from your heart.*

I close my eyes, slow my breathing, and allow the words to come—from somewhere inside me.

"When I was first assigned to restore order in Ferguson, our basic principles were to protect people's ability to make their voices heard. While keeping this community safe, we needed to protect the good people of Ferguson, their businesses, and their property."

I shake my head.

"That's why, earlier tonight, *we* were walking with and listening to the peaceful protesters voicing their frustration in a way that doesn't put others in personal danger."

I start to raise my voice.

"That's also why when we saw violent acts, including shootings, the throwing of Molotov cocktails, and the destruction of businesses, we had to act to protect lives and property."

By "we" I mean *me*. Everyone knows it.

I look back down at my notes and read the account of the night—incident by incident—as if I were reading a police report.

"The situation first started to deteriorate with the shooting of a civilian on West Florissant and Ferguson Avenues at approximately 8:25 p.m. We quickly responded with additional officers to reach the victim and got him to a safe position. That was followed by shots being fired on officers, a number of Molotov cocktails being hurled, and then the looting or vandalism of businesses that included a Domino's Pizza, O'Reilly Auto Parts, a Family Dollar store, and a self-storage business, all on West Florissant."

It's getting worse. Nine days in and it's getting worse. Pain and frustration saturate my voice as I continue to read.

"These were some of the shootings tonight, in addition to the shooting at 8:25 p.m.: One minute later, at 8:26, shots were fired to the north on Canfield. At 8:27, there was a report of a subject down. At 8:28, there was a report of eight people with guns. Tactical teams were dispatched. At 8:56, hundreds of protesters marched toward the Northeast Shopping Center, where we stand at this moment, the site of this command post. As the crowd approached the shopping center, multiple Molotov cocktails were thrown at police. At that time, police deployed tear gas in an attempt to disperse the crowd and stop the violent action. We called in additional support from area police agencies. At 9:15, there was a call for a large crowd gathering at the McDonald's on West Florissant. At 9:20, it was reported that McDonald's was being overrun and employees had locked themselves in the storage room."

I drop my voice, feeling worn out and wasted.

"There were multiple additional reports of Molotov cocktails being thrown. Police were shot at. Makeshift barricades were set up to block police. Bottles and rocks were thrown at police."

I sigh.

"Based on these conditions, I had no alternative but to elevate the level of our response. But to those who would claim that the curfew led to tonight's violence, I will remind you—these incidents began *before* 8:30, three and a half hours before the curfew was to have started last night."

I then talk about a conversation I had earlier with Chief Jon Belmar of the St. Louis County police department, who has returned to assist me, and Chief Sam Dotson of the St. Louis City police department. I report that we are planning additional steps to quiet the violence.

"We are *all* determined to restore peace and safety to the people of Ferguson. And I believe the continued resolve of the good people of this community will ultimately triumph over the few people bent on violence and destruction."

My eyes burning with fatigue, I look up at the members of the media gathered around me. "I have time to take a few questions."

The reporters begin to machine-gun questions at me. I answer the first one I can decipher: "How many people have been injured?"

"We had a couple shooting victims. I think two or three people have been injured," I say, my voice beginning to drone. "We were responding to those shootings. Those shootings that occurred out in the field had nothing to do with law enforcement. They were between people who were actually out on the scene there. They were people who were out on Florissant. There were no officers injured."

Now the questions come so rapid-fire that I can't focus on any of them. The reporters pummel me for information.

How many arrests?

Are you going to bring in the National Guard?

Will you still bring in tanks and shoot tear gas?

By now, I just feel numb. After tonight—after this draining, defeating night of violence, looting, and chaos—I don't see how I can offer any answers or deliver any message that will be informative or helpful. I hear myself giving rote, generic answers. No one benefits from that. I need to go home, regroup, and recharge. I need to put an end to this long, long day. I make the decision to leave the questions unanswered—for now.

"Thank you," I murmur.[2]

Without realizing how fast I've started to move and feeling as if I'm being pulled by a powerful, unseen force, I turn and quickly walk away, reflexively ducking my head as if negotiating a low doorway.

DAY 10

MONDAY, AUGUST 18, 2014

A BULLET HAS NO NAME

God, if you need to take a life—if that will change
everything and stop this—then take mine.

RON JOHNSON

SO MUCH HAPPENS IN A DAY. And when each day stretches into the early hours of the next, time becomes a blur. I'm starting to lose track of what a day *is*.

This past week and a half feels like one long, twenty-four-hour cycle—beginning each morning with hope and faith and promise. But then the dark comes and blots out the light, and the night bursts into flame and fury.

By the time Monday—mercifully—comes to an end, my eyes are glazed over and my vision is cloudy. When I left Ferguson after the nightly news conference, my phone read 3:15 a.m. It must be close to four by now as I drag myself into bed and force my eyes shut. But sleep eludes me again.

Earlier on Monday, a reporter asked me, "Do you see any light at the end of the tunnel?"

"Maybe . . . ," I said, shaking my head. "But as Charles Barkley said, sometimes that light at the end of the tunnel is a train."

★

Not finding sleep, I lie awake and compose another letter to Lori in my mind. The curve of her back rises in sleep next to me, brushing my arm.

What can I say to you?

How can I explain myself to you?

I stretch my neck, lifting my forehead toward the ceiling, and I begin to pray as the tears well up and start flowing down my face.

I was trying to find the easy way out, wasn't I? I was trying to cover both sides of the road. I can't be everywhere at once. I cannot be on both sides. I can only be on my side.

With my chest heaving and sobs wracking my body, I say, "Maybe it's too much."

And then I whisper, "God, I feel like I'm falling off a cliff."

My head throbs as I review the events of the day—starting at the end . . .

★

2:40 a.m.: After another night of violence on the streets of Ferguson, I face the media at my nightly (early morning) news conference. My gait is heavy, and my knees feel rubbery as I walk into a crescent of reporters. They swarm around me, with red lights from the television cameras winking at their backs and cell phones extended toward me at arm's length. A few hard-core veterans of the press corps are still doing it old school, scribbling in their notebooks.

Feeling battered, as if I have just emerged from a raging storm, I ease into a spot behind a long table covered with a lumpy plastic tarp.

A police chaplain to my left bows his head and utters a short prayer. I hear the words, but I can't absorb a single thing he says. As he speaks, my fingers tingle from exhaustion and frayed nerves.

When the chaplain says "Amen," I nod at an officer standing to my right. He yanks the tarp off the table, revealing two handguns and a Molotov cocktail, individually wrapped and taped up in plastic.

I follow the gaze of the reporters as they stare at the guns and the Molotov cocktail. In their collective expression, I read confusion, shock, disbelief. Maybe some of them have never seen a Molotov cocktail this close. Or for that matter, a gun.

I begin to read the notes I've written on the three sheets of paper that flutter in my hands.

"I want to begin by thanking the brave men and women of law enforcement who tonight took another strong step forward in restoring order to the city of Ferguson. Throughout the night, these officers acted with restraint and calm, despite pockets of disorder and coming under violent attack on serveral occasions."[1]

Lying in bed, I picture myself standing in front of those reporters, many who are still staring at the guns and Molotov cocktail and not looking at me.

In my mind, I rewind all the way back to Monday morning.

☆

11:00 a.m.: As I do every morning when I leave for work, I stop at the small built-in desk in our kitchen and slide my "lucky buckeye" into my pocket. I've carried this smooth brown nut—commonly known as a horse chestnut—every day since a friend of mine gave it to me many years ago. I remember him telling me, "Keep it with you. It will bring you luck."

This morning, though, I'm running late, and as I hustle toward the back door, I reach out my hand, but I don't grab the buckeye, which is sitting on the desk right in front of me. Instead, I snatch a cross attached to a string of rosary beads, which is hanging from a tack on the bulletin board over the desk. My son, Brad, left it there months ago.

I don't know why I grab the rosary. I don't do it consciously. I'm not Catholic—I'm a Baptist—and I don't really understand the significance of the rosary or how it's supposed to work. But I reach for the string and take it. A reflex. An instinct. An act of intuition, perhaps. But instantly I feel strangely comforted by the small, twinkling glass pellets. I roll them into my palm, enclosing them with my fingers, and stuff them into my pants pocket.

I look back at the buckeye, sitting right where I always leave it, and I have no second thoughts. Maybe I've lost my belief in luck. Maybe I never had it. Or maybe I've replaced the whole idea of luck with a newfound belief in faith. I don't know. I certainly don't realize at that moment that I have retired my buckeye permanently to the kitchen desk and that I will keep the rosary beads with me for the rest of my days in Ferguson—and longer. Perhaps forever.

To have faith means to believe.

I have faith.

I believe.

But it can be hard.

So very hard.

☆

1:00 p.m.: The governor announces he's lifting the curfew. He has gotten pressure from the NAACP and other groups, who argue that the curfew has obviously not served the intended purpose of quelling the rioting, looting, and violence. In fact, the groups claim, the curfew has served no purpose at all and has caused more harm than good. Honestly, I agree. The curfew had become a lightning rod, an imposed police mandate, giving the protesters another reason to take to the streets and the criminals another excuse for rioting.

All afternoon and into the early evening, I walk. I send out more teams of police, six or seven officers each, whose sole purpose is to mingle and talk with the people on the street. Again, as yesterday, the conversations begin haltingly, awkwardly, uncertainly, a river of ice separating both sides. Gradually, though, a few police officers break the ice and begin talking civilly, even dropping their guard. They abandon their role as police and talk as people. Once again, I witness a few officers laughing with a group of protesters.

Hope.

I may be seeing some hope.

⭐

6:30 p.m.: A man rushes out of the crowd. I recognize him from somewhere. He grabs me by the elbow and steers me toward a car parked off to the side of the road. He swings open the passenger-side door. I lower myself into a crouch and find myself face-to-face with Sister Mary Antona Ebo, a St. Louis legend and civil rights pioneer. Ninety years old and still going strong, she wears her hair cut short, and her brown, button-like eyes shine behind her glasses.

I smile, feeling suddenly humbled and small. "Hello, Sister," I say.

"I've found you," she says.

"Yes . . . ," I say, not sure where this is going.

She takes both my hands. "You say you're going to get things back to normal, but they are not normal." She drills her eyes into mine. "There is no normal. You must change it."

That's all she says.

Sister Mary Antona drops my hands and nods. The man who brought me over reappears, and I stand as he closes the door. He walks around to the driver's side, gets into the car, and drives away, leaving me stunned on the street.

I shout after her, into the air: "Sister, you can't leave me like that."

But she's gone.

☆

I spend the rest of the evening on West Florissant. As I continue to walk, scattered screams of anguish bolt out of nowhere and bore into my skull.

I hear the screams of a mother and father who have lost their son. I hear the screams of people who own businesses that have been burned and looted, their livelihoods destroyed. I hear screams of people who don't feel safe. I hear people screaming, "Why aren't my schools accredited? Why can't I find a job? Why do I feel like a target every day? *Why doesn't anybody care?*"

I hear residents screaming, "Why don't the police respect me?"

I hear police screaming, "Why don't the residents respect me?"

Yes, we're all screaming the same thing.

The pain begins with a scream.

The scream becomes a plea.

The pleas become a conversation.

The conversation leads to understanding.

That is my hope.

There's so much hope and so much promise during the daylight hours.

And then . . .

★

2:40 a.m.: "Tonight began peacefully with calm and orderly protests," I say to the reporters gathered around me. "Other law enforcement officers and I interacted on numerous occasions with protesters who shook hands with officers and expressed their opinions. This is the freedom of expression that we are committed to protect."

I look down at my notes and sigh. "At 9:40 p.m., more than two hundred people walked toward police officers at the corner of West Florissant and Ferguson Avenues. They were loud but not aggressive. They came to the line of police officers, chanted, and then seemed to be turning around and thinning out. Police did not react. In fact, several of the protesters encouraged the crowd to turn around, indicating that their message had been heard."

I swallow. I have to report to the media exactly what happened and in what order. For the second night in a row, I present a detailed police report, an annotation of violence. I list the night's criminal acts. I read them off, one by one, for all to hear. This is my pain. This is my scream.

"But that's when bottles were thrown from the middle and the back of a large crowd that gathered near the media staging area. These criminal acts came from a tiny minority of lawbreakers. But anyone who has been at these protests understands that there is a dangerous dynamic in the night. It allows a small number of violent agitators to hide in the crowd and then attempt to create chaos. The catalyst can be bottles thrown, Molotov cocktails, and of course shots fired. Protesters are peaceful and respectful. Protesters don't clash with police."

My voice grows thick, heavy with hurt. I exhale, my breath causing the page in front of me to flutter.

"In the dark of night, there were at least two people shot."[2]

★

Please, God, don't let there be blood on my hands. This has been my continual prayer, and yet it happens again . . . and again . . . the same insidious pattern. The daylight lulls us all into a sense of comfort, hope, and progress. Then night comes and turns against the day, extinguishing the hope, staining the streets with blood, lighting up the darkness with fire and rage. Gunfire echoes. Buildings burn, crumple, collapse. A battle zone forms. Chaos is unleashed.

I have to control the chaos. That is my job. That is my charge.

I order SWAT trucks in to support the police on the street. I have no choice. I have to protect my officers. I don't see this as an act of aggression. I see it as a last resort.

★

The reporters record, write, and film as I read. "We have been criticized for using SWAT trucks during protests. We did not deploy those into the crowd until things deteriorated. Tonight we used a SWAT truck and another vehicle to get into a violent, dangerous area in order to extract a gunshot victim. . . . Tonight there were numerous reports of shots fired. We also had two fires—one at a business, another at an unoccupied residence. In the area of West Florissant and Canfield, our officers came under heavy gunfire."

My hands shake. I fight to keep the sheets of paper steady. My nerves jangle. Unchecked anger rises into my voice.

"Once again, not a single bullet was fired by officers, despite coming under heavy attack. Four officers were hit by rocks and bottles and sustained injury."

As I look up again, I absently reach into my pocket. My hand encircles the rosary beads. I speak urgently, from the depths of my being.

"I want the good people of this area to come out and protest tomorrow during the daytime hours. Make your voices heard. . . . That is my suggestion."

I hear rustling and throats clearing, and I realize that this statement has startled some of the journalists—and some of the officers—in the room. I hear some people muttering under their breath.

Do I hear the word?

I can't think about that. I can't go there. I fumble with the pages, look down at my notes, search for my place, find it, and press on.

"As of 2:00 a.m., thirty-one people have been arrested tonight. I've said that many of the criminal element that have been coming through Ferguson are not from this area. Tonight, some of those arrested came from as far away as New York and California."

I flip to the next page, pausing briefly to glance at my notes. I can no longer focus on what I have written. I speak off the cuff, from the heart.

"I want to address the role of the media in what is going on here. Tonight, the media had to be repeatedly asked to return to the sidewalks and get out of the street when clashes were going on in the street. We need to have those areas cleared. This is a matter of your safety and the safety of others. We need the roads cleared so we can reach people who need us. Please clear the roads when asked. Please pay attention to the officers. Let's pay attention to those who are protesting peacefully. Let's not glamorize the acts of criminals."

I suddenly feel worn down. Raw to the bone. If I were alone, my emotions would overflow and I would lose it.

You can't do that, I tell myself. *You can't fall apart here.*

I take a moment to compose myself, and my gaze wanders to the table in front of me with the guns and the Molotov cocktail. My voice raspy, I say, "On this table you see two guns that we confiscated tonight. These guns were in vehicles right near this media area where you are standing. On this table you also see a Molotov cocktail that was thrown tonight. I have talked to many of you in the media who said that you have not seen any of these thrown. I wanted to show you."

Several reporters step forward. They lean over the table, zoom in, and snap pictures of the weapons. I lose myself for a few seconds in the scribbling and scratching of pens, the clicking of cell phone cameras, and the whir of photos being posted to the Internet.

"We did not have a curfew tonight," I say. "As a matter of fact, we told some of the protesters that they could stay as long as they wanted. But after midnight, safety became a concern. We had officers who were in the midst of gunfire."

Maybe it's the lateness of the hour or the frustration of the day, but my voice cracks as sheer emotion claws its way into my throat. I sniff, desperately trying not to unravel in the middle of this press conference.

"I guarantee you that those officers' wives and husbands and parents are calling them now to see if—"

I swallow and breathe. I can't fight it anymore. I allow the tears to come. I speak haltingly.

"I stood there and listened over the radio and heard the screams of the officers who were under gunfire. . . . We can't have this. We do not want any citizen hurt. We do not want any officer hurt. But when you're shooting in apartment complexes and children are lying in their beds and bullets are flying everywhere. . . . There's an old saying on the street: 'A bullet has no name.' We do not want to lose another life in this community."[3]

I'm done. I can't talk anymore. The reporters, sensing that I've come to the end of my prepared statement, barrage me with questions. I hear them, but I cannot comprehend them. The words come to me as garbled fragments, as if the reporters were speaking a foreign language. The one question that burns in my mind is my own: *Has anyone seen my tears, felt my emotion?*

And then out of the cacophony of voices I hear someone ask about accidentally arresting members of the media or mistaking members of the media for protesters. I feel compelled to address that issue.

"In the midst of chaos, when officers are running around, we're not sure who's a journalist and who's not. And yes, if I see somebody with a fifty-thousand-dollar camera on his shoulder, I'm pretty sure. But some journalists are walking around and all you have is a cell phone because you're from a small media outlet; some of you may just have a camera around your neck. So, yes we are—we may take some of you into custody."

More rustling. I can almost feel the discomfort rising.

Did he really just say that?

Well, I did promise that above all I would be honest. So there you have it.

"When that happens," I continue, "if we do take you in and we find out you're a journalist, we take the proper action. But in the midst of chaos, we have to be safe. We're trying to keep you safe. We're providing protection for journalists. We had a journalist who was trapped in the midst of that gunfire, and we're providing protection for them. We took journalists back to their trucks."

I lower my head, reach into my pocket, and grip the rosary beads. When I lift my eyes again, I speak with a conviction that startles everyone around me.

"I'm going to tell you: This nation is watching each and every one of us. This nation is watching law enforcement. This nation is watching our media. If we're going to solve this, we're going to have to do it together. I want you to think about that tonight. We are going to have to do it *together*."

I don't fully hear the next question, but I understand the intent. It is the same question that has been keeping me up at night, the question that will still haunt me even years after this is over. Maybe nobody even asks the question. Maybe I just keep hearing it reverberating in my own mind.

You allowed businesses to be looted. Should you have stopped that?

"I talked to one journalist today," I say. "He talked about us using SWAT vehicles and wearing SWAT outfits. He told me that the other night he stood in that line, with those businesses being looted. He was saying that we cannot rebound from that night; families saying that they lost their livelihoods; the media saying we did not do enough."

I look straight ahead, avoiding everyone's eyes, feeling my tears come.

"I stood on that line and officers were crying. Officers were angry at me for standing on that line and letting that happen. Today, some of those officers walked by me because they're hurt. They're ashamed that we stood there."

The faces in front of me disappear. I see only blank circles of flesh. I am suddenly alone, standing by myself, my hand in my pocket, clutching the rosary beads, talking into the wind.

"I'm telling you—we're going to make this neighborhood whole. We are going to make this community whole. And we're going to do it together. *We are going to do this together*."[4]

That is my goal—to bring peace to this community and do it together.

How can we do this?

There is only one way. One path.

Faith.

Faith in each other.

Faith in sharing our community.

Faith in humanity.

Faith in God.

That is our path.

We must have faith.

"God," I say, under my breath, "please let them hear me."

Their questions spin around me, pound into me. I can't grasp the words. I feel myself slowly pivoting from the reporters. I am not dismissing them. I just don't have it in me to answer one more question.

"Have a good night," I say quietly.

That isn't just lip service. I mean it.

Please. Have a good night.

And if you will, Lord, give us a good day.

DAY 11

TUESDAY, AUGUST 19, 2014

MAN,
BLACK MAN,
TROOPER

The destroyers will rarely be held accountable.

TA-NEHISI COATES
BETWEEN THE WORLD AND ME

AFTER THE MONDAY NIGHT press conference, I manage to get three hours of sleep.

All fitful and not in a row.

Late Tuesday morning, I stop at the desk in the kitchen on my way out, remove the rosary beads from the bulletin board, and thread them through my fingers. I hold them up to the light, nestled in a small mound in my hand, and a sense of calm comes over me. Other than my time on SWAT, I have always worked alone, patrolled alone, walked alone. Since taking over the responsibility for security in Ferguson, I've felt even more alone than ever. But as I look at these beads in my hand, I know that I'm not alone. I have a partner.

☆

Two pieces of wisdom live within me, embrace me, blanket me like a shadow, keep me focused, keep me strong.

Faith is not what you feel. It's what you do.

I read that somewhere once.

Trouble doesn't last always.

I've heard that often.

It's my mother's favorite expression.

I know I'm on a journey. I know also that every journey comes to an end.

☆

Again, I walk. The crowd today fills in quicker and seems larger than any I remember. Different groups, different affiliations—church groups, citizens' groups, people from Amnesty International, LGBT groups, pockets of paid protesters.

Reporters walk with us. Camera crews track us, tail us. News helicopters hover, and the whack-whack-whack of their blades supply the backbeat to sporadic chanting: "Hands up; don't shoot!" and "I am Michael Brown!" People use their cell phones to broadcast up-to-the-minute news reports, with only a momentary delay before they're posted to YouTube or Facebook. I can watch myself live, walking on West Florissant.

"Look at this," a female news anchor says from within a small rectangle in the corner of the screen. "These are protesters walking in the middle of the street. They are with a police escort after so many nights of violence. The Missouri State Highway Patrol is handling the policing of these protesters. KMBC's Eli Rosenberg is live from the streets of Ferguson. Eli, are you seeing anything different from police?"

An excitable young man in a rumpled blue shirt stands to the side with a group of people. He holds a microphone and gestures toward the crowd.

"You guys can see where the protesters have gathered," Eli says. "They have been marching all day. It is such a different feeling here. We just got a briefing from Ron Johnson, the captain from the Missouri State Highway Patrol, who is leading the security here in Ferguson. He told us—"

Eli shakes his head. For a moment he seems struck mute. He swallows, gathers himself, and continues.

"Just a *totally different* feeling today going into tonight. Officers will be here, but they will not be wearing gas masks like they have in days past."

The camera pans through the crowd, landing on a group of police officers standing in the center of the road. They are in uniform, some wearing short sleeves because of the heat. They stand in a cluster, surveying the crowd, hands on hips. A few talk with protesters. If you had no idea what had occurred over the past few days—if you had been traveling in space or recently awakened from a coma—you might think you were watching a parade, a rally, or a tailgate party.

"We've seen fewer officers than we have before," Eli says. "The ones we have seen have not been heavily armed. They've just been wearing their regular uniforms as if they were on patrol. These people you see have been marching up and down the street all afternoon and are getting an escort from the man himself leading security, Captain Ron Johnson. He was in the front of this line. He says he wouldn't ask his troopers to do anything he wasn't willing to do. It is really an impressive display when you see all these people out here. They say they have come from all over. We've talked to people who have come from Chicago and Atlanta. They saw what happened last night, but they say they are not deterred by the violence. They want to march peacefully, and Captain Johnson says he will provide that security as long as they are here."

★

I walk, but sometimes I feel as if my legs are striding on a mysterious, unseen conveyor belt. I'm unconscious of traveling, of even taking *steps*. I start off at one point and before I know it, I've arrived somewhere else, a half mile away. It's as if I've been caught up in a raging sea, swept up in a ferocious current of humanity. It feels both unsettling and magical.

I don't fear this current. I welcome walking in these waters.

Moving rapidly forward, I arrive at the far end of West Florissant and prepare to loop back.

"There are hundreds of people here," Eli Rosenberg reports in the local television coverage. "This is right outside the QuikTrip that was burned out Sunday night. People we've talked to say they really want to change the message that has been portrayed in the media of all the violence. All these people gathered here—people as far as the eye can see—and people are still coming in."

★

To go home.

That's every police officer's goal.

It should be *everyone's* goal.

It should be a reasonable expectation.

I speak with a frantic woman, who points at the crowd amassed on the opposite side of the street.

"Last night, I was walking with my son," she says. "He's eighteen years old. And we were walking together."

She wags her finger in frustration.

"We couldn't get home. I could not get my son home. He is not a looter. We were out here marching—"

She interrupts herself, her eyes wide.

"You ask us to go home at night, but some of us *can't get home.*"

"I understand," I say. "We have to take care of that."

"I'm not talking about the police," she says. "People were shooting *at the police.*"

"Chaos," I say.

"We're caught in the middle," she says.

We look into the crowd, at the cross section of people walking with us—young; old; black; white; clergy; men in work clothes; men in button-down shirts; shirtless young men wearing red bandannas over their faces, revealing only their eyes; young women pushing strollers; people holding signs; families holding hands.

"Maybe my son seems old to some people, but in the world, he's young. He's innocent."

The woman looks into the crowd. "He's lost his innocence. Some adults have lost their innocence too."

"Chaos," I repeat.

"That's right."

"You know what comes after chaos?" I say. "Calm."

The woman's eyes widen, glisten. I see a glimmer of hope.

☆

I get a phone call telling me that Attorney General Eric Holder has come to Ferguson and wants to see me. We arrange to meet at a small neighborhood restaurant. I arrive a few minutes early.

I hear that he's come to offer his support, to validate the choices I've made. But I can't help feeling nervous, almost as if I'd been called out of class to see the principal or had been told that my father wants to have a talk. This meeting makes these days feel so *real*—and momentous.

The door to the restaurant opens and a couple of grim-faced, big-shouldered, sunglass-wearing Secret Service guys step inside. They scan the place, and a few seconds later, one of them opens the door. The attorney general walks in and approaches me.

"My man," he says.

"How you doing, sir?"

"You are the man," he says, extending his hand.

"We're trying to make it right," I say, shaking his hand. "Trying to make it better."

The attorney general pulls me into an embrace. "This is what policing should be," he whispers. "You're making a real difference."

"Thank you, sir."

He pulls away and looks me in the eye. "Today seems a little better, huh?"

"Well, yes, the community has come out. The elders have come out. The clergy has come out. Everyone's talking, interacting."

"That's what makes a difference," Mr. Holder says. "Allowing people to express themselves. And getting the police involved with the community."

"That's what we have to do."

"Well, you're doing it."

"It's a game of inches," I say.

"Inches," he says, nodding, trying out the word.

"Yes," I say. "Moving forward by inches. Inch by inch."

"*Inches*," Attorney General Holder says.

★

After the attorney general leaves, I return to the command post. I walk among the officers, some of whom support me and some of whom resent me, and I realize that—no matter what—we have to coexist. We have to share the same space—emotional space as well as physical space. That has to happen in all our communities. We must embrace a simple, basic tenet that every child learns in kindergarten: *You have to share.*

Out on the streets of Ferguson, I see many people sharing one cause, one hope, one space, but I also see others who have taken spaces for themselves or for self-gain. They want to bring attention to themselves, or they want to riot.

Why?

I struggle to find reasons. Maybe they feel oppressed and simply want to express themselves. Maybe they want to cause trouble because trouble is all they know. Maybe they're just criminals.

I see all types of people on the street now. I see professional protest leaders—people who actually teach others how to protest, how to march, where to march, what to say, and what not to say. I see police who refuse to engage with protesters, who resent them—and *me.* With some officers and certain protesters, I see no attempt from either side to connect.

I don't allow my spirits to sag—there's nothing to gain in that. If that's where we are today, then that's where we are. I hear my mother's words, "What good would it do?" If a police officer can't do good for people, then who can? Who will?

I continue to walk, with my head up and my hopes high.

Inch by inch, I told Attorney General Holder. If we advance only an inch today, I'll take it. I'll take whatever I can get.

I walk down the middle of that road—a road that is both literal and symbolic. Police on one side, protesters on the other. I am embraced by people on both sides. I'm ostracized by others. I belong on both sides, but for now I don't want to choose either one. So I walk in the middle, and the assurance of my stride rises and falls, ebbs and flows. Some moments feel like a treacherous climb up a steep peak. Other moments feel easy, even joyous— like I'm on a slow, peaceful stroll that dips into a lush, green valley. I try to find something positive in every moment. I focus on that one thing and try to string several of those moments together. Sometimes I can't find enough positive to fill even a moment. I find only a blip, lasting barely a nanosecond. Still, I have to find something—and so I walk toward what I believe will be the good, the positive. I walk into the unknown.

Inch by inch.

Moment by moment.

That's how we'll get there.

★

I walk, looking on both sides of the street. Across the way, I see police officers who have spoken up against me, expressing strong opposition. They don't agree with me or with anything about me—my command, my authority, my philosophy, my tactics, the color of my skin. When I first took over as head of security in Ferguson, I ignored them. I pushed their argumentative words or ugly silence out of my mind. I refused to allow their hostility to affect me.

Since I've started carrying the rosary beads, things have changed. I feel a sense of warmth flitting through me, almost like a spiritual pulse, lightening my step and illuminating my perspective. I still don't appreciate these officers' negativity, but I acknowledge it and accept it. As the saying goes, *It takes all kinds.* Like me, these officers wear the badge proudly. We may have different, opposing ideas, but I need them on my side. We need each other. We are in this together.

I no longer ignore these officers. I now seek them out. If I'm walking and I see an officer turn his back on me, I'll break out of the crowd, go over to the officer, and offer my hand. "How you doing?" I'll say. "You all right?"

Reluctantly—and not always the first time I try—these officers turn and face me and shake my hand.

"Let me know if I can do anything for you," I say, finding one officer's eyes. "I want to help you if I can. I also want to tell you that I appreciate what you're doing. I appreciate your being out here."

The next time I'm walking, when I see that officer, I tip my cap to him. He glares back for a second, but then he tips his cap to me.

Inch by inch . . .

I talk to the protesters about the police. I explain that most police only want to protect people's freedom. These officers are good people, I tell them.

"Give them a chance," I say. "They want the night to end the same way you do. They want to get home safe."

Keep your head up, I tell myself, my fingers wrapped around my rosary beads. *Believe in small victories. You may not see any victories now, but those small victories will come.*

At a meeting in a church, I speak to an older gentleman.

"We all have failures," he says. "Every day. We fail every day."

I need to understand that. I need to embrace and expect that. I have to recognize these failures, learn from them, and get better.

I am beginning to understand others' opposition, and even their fear.

We have entered a new moment—all of us. We have never been in this moment before. This is all new territory.

I pray that we will never be here again.

★

I walk.

I feel so . . . humbled.

I feel so small.

I feel that I have stepped away from being a policeman.

I'm just a man.

The racial slurs fly at me from both sides, from all sides.

Criminals in the crowd call me the word because I'm The Man.

Cops patrolling the crowd call me the word because I'm a black man.

But I'm just a man.

★

Don Lemon interviews me on CNN. We stand on a street corner.

"Let's be real," Don says.

Over these few days, now totaling almost a week, Don and I have spent time together, on camera and off, and have become friends. I trust him to be honest and fair. He trusts me to tell him the truth. Off the air, we talked about the importance of getting this story out to the nation, to the world. I feel that Ferguson will ultimately be an example of something terrible that will evolve into something good. I believe that.

Don, hands on hips, says, "We hear people saying, '*We're pissed off*' and '*F the police.*' People calling you words like *coon*. People calling you a sellout . . . because you want peace. I'm sure you've heard that."

Hearing Don speak those words makes me bristle. I feel my already-straight back draw up, become even straighter. "I've heard it," I say. "And that is untrue. I wear this uniform, but it defines me at a low level. I'm a man first. I'm a black man second. I'm a husband. I'm a father. I'm a son. A trooper? I am a lot of things before I am a trooper. But one thing I am is an honest man."

I lean toward Don. I know what I'm saying is being broadcast to the world. I want the world to hear.

"I have my integrity. I will stand up for what is right. And even if this uniform is wrong, I will stand for what's right. If this uniform is wrong, I'll tell you we're wrong."

Don gestures at the street, at a boarded-up storefront. "Are you embarrassed by any of this?"

I wait for a count of *one—two—three* . . .

"Yes," I say. "I think everybody who is a good citizen of this community, this state, and this nation is embarrassed. Yes."

☆

Sometimes it gets to be too much.

I close myself in my sanctuary, the bathroom. I pray and I cry. I cry and I pray.

I pull myself together and go back out there.

I don't reveal my emotions to anyone—not to Lori, not to anyone on the force. I keep my feelings locked up. To all observers, I show strength and resolve and humanity. That's what I try to show most. Humanity. We cannot come to the end of this endless day until we walk together. We may want—and need—different things. But we have to walk together.

Literally.

Spiritually.

Faithfully.

★

Late in the day, before darkness sets, I sit in the truck with a few of my guys. We lounge, nobody speaking, four guys on a break. Then without warning a wave of exhaustion levels all of us at once. A couple of the guys bob their heads, fighting sleep, then lose the battle and nod off. I tell myself I'll doze for only a minute. I'll take a five-minute power nap. I feel my eyes grow heavy as I drift off. After a while, I jerk awake, my back sore, my eyes blinking.

"How long was I out?"

"About forty minutes, Captain."

"Wow."

I yawn away the grogginess and step out of the truck. My body feels refreshed. Forty minutes is all I get. Forty minutes is all I need. Crazy.

Groups of attorneys arrive. They instruct protesters on their rights, their actions, how to stand, where to stand, what to say, when to retreat, how to resist arrest. They wear green hats. They scrutinize the police. They tell the protesters, "If something happens, we're here. We're watching."

People hand out fliers and other literature. Some people sell buttons, hats, T-shirts. Politicians arrive with entourages. People from the LGBT community march, sing, chant, and give interviews whenever possible, whenever asked, talking about the hostility and prejudice they face. The streets are now overflowing with people who are hoping the media—especially the national media—will pick them out and shine a light on their cause, give attention to their struggles.

Truckloads of food roll in. Volunteers pass out prepackaged meals, drinks, protein bars, vitamin supplements, heat tablets. People in the crowd grab the food and tear open the packages as if they haven't eaten in a week. In some cases, that may be the truth. I watch people distributing the food to lines of protesters and I think, *Am I really seeing this? Is this real? The protest is being catered?*

I walk.

A woman approaches and walks with me stride for stride.

"I was at Greater Grace Church, Captain Johnson," she says. "I heard your speech. I heard you say that Michael Brown's life would make things better for your son, for all our sons. Do you still believe that?"

"Yes," I say after a while, thrown by the bluntness of her question. "I do. I do think it will get better." I pause and hold her gaze. "It has to."

★

Tonight, it doesn't get better.

It gets worse.

With the National Guard massed behind us, a military presence looming just down the road—not mobilized but on alert, an indelible visual of how the night overruns the day—we arrest forty-seven people, bringing our two-day, Monday/Tuesday total to seventy-eight arrests.

At 2:49 a.m., I walk to the area outside the command post to deliver my nightly news conference. Well, my early-Wednesday-morning news conference.

With six officers fanned out behind me, I face the press corps. I haven't jotted down notes or written a statement. I look at the cluster of media reps jockeying for position in front of me, and I feel that tonight I should just answer their questions. I mutter quietly, "Good evening. I should say, 'Good morning.' Because you've all been privy to tonight's events, I will dispense with a statement and just take your questions."

The questions come at me high and hard, like fastballs. The first question I hear is about our decision to use tear gas and pepper spray. I lower my voice, speaking as patiently as I can.

"We have a shooting victim who is in critical condition, who may lose her life. We had a subject standing in the middle of the road waving a handgun. We had a police car shot at tonight. Yes, I think that was the proper response to maintain officer safety—and public safety—so we didn't have more victims, whether they were law enforcement or some of our citizens."

As the questions come at me from all sides and every angle, I start to feel like a hockey goalie, crouching with my glove up and my stick at the ready, trying to protect the net from one vicious shot after another.

From the right: "Do you have any more information on the victim?"

"We know the victim is in critical condition, and the victim is a male."

From the left: "Do you have any idea where the gunshots came from?"

"We do not. We were responding to the person who was shot, providing assistance. The shooting was on West Florissant."

From point-blank range: "Any information on the shooter?"

"No. I've given you all the information I have on the shooting at this time. St. Louis County is in the process of an investigation—"

Right side: "Was the shooting victim transported to the hospital in a protester's car? That's what we heard."

"Yes. By the time we responded down there, some other protesters had loaded the victim into their car. They did call us. Our command post officers were in contact with them, and they told us where they were going to take the victim."

Left side: "What were the charges?"

"Failure to disperse."

Up the middle, in the back: "Did you apprehend the man who had the gun?"

"No, we didn't. We did observe him running off as we approached."

Left side, back: "Your response was to—?"

"Our response was to what was happening at Red's Barbecue. That's what our response was."

Back right: "Were you responding to a 9-1-1 call?"

"I don't know how the call came in. We were in contact with the parties who were there with the victim."

Right side: "Was there any looting tonight?"

"Not that we know of. We had officers all along West Florissant, and we did not observe any broken glass or any damage to buildings, and we didn't receive any alarm calls."

Directly in front: "Did the tear gas come before or after the shots were fired?"

"The tear gas came as we approached Red's Barbecue and we encountered the subject who had the weapon, and then he ran off."

Same reporter, directly in front: "The operation began before he—"

I interrupt to clarify: "We got intelligence that subjects had entered Red's Barbecue and that they were armed. When we got there, several subjects ran as we approached."

Left side: "Were there any other reports of shots fired? We heard that."

"Yes. I was out there and I did hear several gunshots fired in the air while we were standing out front."

After this question, I feel myself sag, my patience fray. I've hit the wall. I can't answer another question. I'm afraid I will speak gibberish. Colonel Ron Replogle, flanking me on the left, sees my eyes glazing over. He steps forward.

"I have to get my captain to bed tonight, so let's take two more questions, and then I'm getting him out of here."

Two more questions.

Just two more . . .

A woman on the left side, shouting to be heard, asks about reports of a fire down on West Florissant near Canfield. "Was there a fire?"

"There was not," I say.

And then I hear a rather kind male voice, low, on the right side: "It's almost three in the morning. What can we expect the rest of the night and into daybreak?"

Maybe it's because I know this is the last question of the night, or maybe it's the reporter's gentle voice, but his question lifts me up. I locate him on the right-hand side and look into his eyes.

"I expect that we will still patrol the area. We will have officers patrolling the area throughout the night to make sure our citizens are safe and our businesses remain healthy. Our businesses *have* to remain healthy. I talked to many citizens out there today who say that they have nowhere to go to get the things they need. So the businesses have to remain healthy."

I feel my pulse racing. I pause to catch my breath. I count silently to three and then say, "I can tell you that prior to tonight's violence—about nine or ten o'clock—I was down there and several people came up to me and said they would stand in front of those businesses and protect those businesses. If those citizens are prepared to protect those businesses, then the police are willing to stand there too. Thank you very much."

I turn away from the podium and practically sprint to my car. It is well past 3:00 a.m.

The endless day continues.

DAY 12

WEDNESDAY, AUGUST 20, 2014

"WHERE HAVE YOU BEEN?"

Fall in your ways, so you can sleep at night;
Fall in your ways, so you can wake up and rise.

SOLANGE KNOWLES
"RISE"

AS I PULL INTO OUR DRIVEWAY, my heart sinks. Lori has turned on every light in the house. I panic.

Why would she leave every light on?

Something must have happened.

Has someone come to my house?

Did someone try to break in?

I bolt out of the car and fling open the front door.

Lori stands in the doorway of the living room. She's wearing her robe tight around her nightclothes and her arms are folded. She does not look happy. She looks the opposite of happy. She looks angry.

"You're up," I say. That was about as lame an opening line as anyone could possibly utter, until I follow it with "Is something wrong?"

"Yes, there is something wrong."

Enunciating every word. Not a good sign.

"Okay . . ."

"You know I watch the coverage."

She unfolds her arms, slams her fists onto her hips, and cocks her head slightly.

Yep. Angry. Really angry.

Good police work, Ron.

I stumble as I try to speak. "So, what . . . ah . . . what's—"

"What's *wrong*? People are shooting at police—shooting up police cars—and you're out there on the front lines walking without your *vest*?"

"Well, all right, see—"

"Do not tell me you forgot it."

"No. I didn't forget it."

Pause.

I'm about to lose big-time here.

"I didn't have it."

Lori bites her lip. I'm not sure whether she's about to laugh, scream, or cry.

I take a tentative step forward. "Things happened so quickly, the dynamics out there changed so fast that I didn't have time to get it."

She starts to speak and shakes her head. I take another step forward and gently touch her shoulder. She lets me leave my hand there. She's softening. I'm wearing her down. Plus, it's 3:30 in the morning.

"I've been a wreck," she says.

"I'll keep it with me from now on. I'll keep it close by. I promise."

"You better," she says.

"I will. I'm sorry."

She nods and a tear trickles down her cheek. I reach over and dab it away with my thumb.

"I'm really sorry," I say again. "I know you're angry."

"I am angry," she says. "And I'm scared."

We grab each other, hug, and hold on, clinging as if we hadn't seen each other in weeks, which is what it feels like.

"You must be exhausted," Lori whispers.

"No," I say, my eyes closing heavily. "I'm way past exhausted."

Before I get into bed, I stop to pray. I go into the bathroom and close the door. Lowering my head and placing my hands over my eyes, I thank God for giving me the strength to go on. I thank him for my resolve. I thank him for keeping me together as I walk down the middle of that road of pain and strife—with the police condemning me on one side and protesters clamoring at me on the other. I thank God for letting me walk with my head held high and my heart open. I don't ask for anything, except for the strength to continue.

☆

Wednesday morning, I wake up before the alarm. As I lie in bed for a few seconds, adjusting to the darkness in the room, I suddenly feel . . . *different*. Everything around me—every object in the room—is unchanged, familiar, comforting. But there's a different energy. The atmosphere seems more peaceful somehow, as if a long, stormy night has given way to the first fleeting rays of sunlight. I ease out of bed, careful not to wake Lori, and pad into the bathroom. Before I wash up, I drop my head into my hands and say out loud, "Something's happening. Something different. I can feel it." And then I whisper to God, "Thank you."

At the breakfast table, I sip orange juice and watch the local television coverage, switching between stations. I think about the people sitting at home every day who watch the events in Ferguson, the violence and chaos unfolding on their TV screens. I think about the families of police officers who watch and worry about their sons and daughters and brothers and sisters reporting to duty and danger in the midst of the unrest and chaos. I think about my wife and my kids. I can feel their concern hanging on me, almost like an extra layer of skin as I leave the house for Ferguson every morning.

And I think about the parents whose sons and daughters leave home each morning to join the protests—and how they must watch the coverage in fear, petrified by what they see happening on the streets of their community, where they shop, where they eat, where they live.

I realize that I must speak to them and *for* them. I have been given the privilege to touch their lives. I am their voice. I have been allowed to have an impact on them. I am revealing these days to them. I am revealing myself to them. I believe that I am delivering a positive message from my heart—hoping and praying that my message touches *their* hearts.

This is our moment, I tell myself. Then I remember what a store owner said to me the other day: "This is not a *moment*. This is a *movement*."

It would be a disservice for me not to at least try to connect to those people at home, as well as to the people on the street. As the conflict continues to rage, I keep hearing these words: "We need to see a difference. We need to try to create a partnership and an understanding. This is our time."

I believe what I said at Greater Grace Church on Sunday about

Michael Brown's death making a difference. That hope has become a prayer that I repeat on my knees at home and while clutching the sink in the command post bathroom: *Please don't let Michael Brown's death be in vain. Please don't let us have a tragedy without a purpose.*

★

I'm standing on the street, across from Don Lemon—on national television, midinterview. He grins at me. I don't like that grin. I sense a good-natured trap. I smile at Don, bracing for the question I know he's about to ask.

"So," he says, "are you still married?"

I glance down at my hands, steeple my fingers, and crack a smile. I told Don earlier, off the air, about my conversation with Lori last night. He asked if he could talk about it during our interview, and I told him it was all right.

"Yes," I tell the world on camera. "I'm still married."

Don flashes that grin again.

"Because we understand that your wife was not happy with you," he says.

"She was not happy with me last night," I reply before briefly recounting the story. I end by saying, "I promised her I would have the vest close by from now on. So tonight she can get some sleep, and she won't have to yell at me when I get home."

Don laughs and then quickly shifts his tone, turning serious, almost grim. "Do you have a message to the people who are out here?"

I silently count to three before answering—to gather my thoughts and measure my tone.

"Yes. My message to the people who are out here: *We will get through this.* And to the agitators: *You will not defeat us.*"

There was a time, before Ferguson, when I kept the media at arm's length. I considered them somewhere between my enemy and a distant relative. That's changed. I now take every opportunity to talk to reporters because I know we need the media's help. They can show scenes of hope and understanding and partnership. It's easy to show the looting and fires and tear gas and the National Guard lined up with their military vehicles. It's easy to broadcast images of crowds of people shrouded in clouds of tear gas. Rule number one of broadcast news: *If it bleeds, it leads.* I get that. It's what draws an audience.

People may be more drawn to footage of cops descending on a criminal who is clawing at his eyes after being pepper-sprayed than footage of a cop and a protester hugging. But both images are real.

People need to see both.

☆

Today, like every day for the past week, I walk.

That is my plan. My strategy.

I walk. I talk. I listen.

What happened last night doesn't matter. Today is a new day, a new beginning. I have to erase last night's chaos and start fresh. I walk twice a day, at least. I want the people to see that I am here no matter what. I am here. I am here for *them.* I will not abandon them. I will protect their freedom to be on the street and to protest. I want them to protest without fear. I don't want them to be afraid of the police. I don't want them to be afraid of me. I want them to know me and trust me.

Eventually.

For now, I'll settle for having them know that I'm here.

Today as I walk, I experience the same feeling I had when I woke up: *Something's different.* I can't put my finger on it. I can't quantify it. I don't really notice anything out of the ordinary . . . and then . . . I start to see small things. People who haven't talked to me before nod. People acknowledge that I've come back and that I keep coming back, every day, as I promised I would when I spoke at the church.

"I'll see you out there," I said.

"You're out here."

I hear that phrase couched in surprise, appreciation—even gratitude.

I want to send a clear message . . . and I want to hammer it home.

We're going to get through this together. And *I'm not going anywhere.*

So I walk.

☆

I start to see a difference, and I start to hear things change.

The first time I walked, some people shouted, "You don't want to hear what I have to say! Get away! You don't want to hear me!"

Now when I walk, everyone wants to talk to me—really talk.

I stop and I listen.

They tell me about their struggles; they list their complaints; they express their anger and their frustration, some of it pent up for years. And I listen. When they finish, I respond to what they've said. And *they* listen.

We have begun a conversation.

Police and the people, talking on the street.

That's all it is.

But it's a change.

As police officers, we can't be satisfied with just *engaging* with the community. We have to become *part* of the community. We have to *be* the community.

"I am here" and "I am you" must merge into "I am here *for you*."

★

I walk in the August heat, my uniform shirt soaked in sweat. I've started bringing a second shirt and hanging it in the command post so that I can change shirts after my first walk of the day. As I walk, more and more people hand me towels to dry my face. The same woman comes out every day and pats my forehead and neck with her towel. The towel looks a little unsanitary, but the gesture is beautiful, and that overrides everything else. I feel I'm sharing in her sweat and in her tears.

People continue to hand me bottles of water. One woman, holding a sign that suggests something rather crude be done to the police, sees me and shouts, "Hey, you need to make sure you stay hydrated! Get him some water. Get the captain a cold bottle of water!"

Conversations form the beginnings of relationships. A woman comes up to me and says, "Do you remember me?"

"Of course I do," I say. "I've seen you every day."

She looks at me, stunned. I don't think she believes me. Maybe she's never had a friendly exchange with a police officer before.

"*Do* you remember me?" she asks again, unconvinced. "Really?"

"I really do," I say as I take her hand. "I've seen you out here. You've been here from the beginning. Now I'm here today, I was here yesterday, and I'll be here tomorrow."

"You do remember me," she says.

The voices change. The sounds change. The tone changes. The thickness in the air lifts. The ache I hear softens. The throbbing pain I've felt thrumming through the community eases. Days ago, when I first walked down the street, people shouted, "We didn't ask you to walk down here! What do you want?"

Now I hear, "Where have you been?"

I talk and I listen. I listen more than I talk. I try to *hear* more than listen. When I do speak, I speak from my heart, from my soul. Words are important, words are real, but our words matter less than we think. Actions matter more.

Interacting on the street with the protesters.

Listening.

Walking.

Being seen.

Being here.

At first I didn't know what I should do. I didn't know how to make that connection. But I had faith. I held on to that. Gradually I learned that faith is not a feeling. Faith is not what you say. Faith is not even what you believe. Faith is what you do.

I walk all day until it starts to get dark. Dusk eases in with a sense of foreboding, bringing on the night. As we've seen, day after day, night seems to bring out the rioters, the violence. I fear the night.

Every night before our briefings, I pray. Tonight, like this morning, I don't ask God for anything. I simply thank him for the change I feel, for the change that's coming. I thank him that the storm finally seems to be breaking. And then I take a deep breath, walk out of my sanctuary, and take on the night.

✬

The change I felt this morning carried throughout the day. But now comes the true test. I gear up for what might happen tonight. I keep my vest close by. But the night surprises me. This night is different. We experience a few unruly moments, some disruption, a little bit of chaos. But we have noticeably less violence, the unrest is not as loud, and there's less rage in the air. I feel it: the shift, the break in the storm. In the words of Sam Cooke's classic song "A Change Is Gonna Come," "It's been a long—a long time comin', but I know a change gonna come, oh yes it will."

The media gather at two in the morning. I've jotted a few notes, and my eyes are burning and blurry from strain. I wear my glasses. I begin to speak, and I only occasionally glance at the paper in my hand. I wait for a moment to allow the members of the media to settle. I speak evenly, my voice level, sounding more controlled than I feel.

"Twenty-four hours ago, I told you how organized and increasingly violent instigators were inserting themselves into law-abiding protesters. I asked that the forces for peace come out and protest before the sun went down so that they would not serve as shields for the lawbreakers in the night."

My voice begins to rise, but I want to tamp down the excitement I'm starting to feel, so I swallow before I continue.

"Tonight we saw a different dynamic. Protest crowds were a bit smaller and they came out earlier. We had to respond to fewer incidents than the night before. There were no Molotov cocktails tonight. There were no shootings."

I look at the notes I've scribbled and start to read. I hear myself speak, almost as if I'm in the crowd, my voice suddenly solemn, weighty.

"A vehicle did approach the command center, and threats were made to kill a police officer. We identified the vehicle, located it, and made arrests. We seized two loaded handguns. In another incident, a third loaded handgun was also seized. At about midnight, bottles were thrown at police officers near a public storage business located on West Florissant. This forced police to deploy their helmet shields for protection and then break into the crowd and search for the agitators, who hid behind the media for safety."

I look up, search the faces of the press corps in front of me, and catch the eye of one of the reporters. He seems to see the relief I feel. I force back a tiny smile.

One night, I think. *It was one night and it wasn't perfect—not by a long shot; but it felt different . . .*

I fold up my notes and speak quietly.

"All night and early this morning, no smoke bombs and no tear gas were used by police. We did deploy very limited pepper spray. And tonight, once again, no police officer fired a single bullet."

I nod, finished with the briefing.

One night, I think.

That's how this will end.

With one good night.

DAY 13

THURSDAY, AUGUST 21, 2014

"TROUBLE DOESN'T LAST ALWAYS"

---

*Faith is taking the first step, even when you
don't see the whole staircase.*

MARTIN LUTHER KING, JR.

I STAND IN MY BATHROOM at home and look at myself in the mirror. My eyes look sunken and red. As I study my reflection and let my mind run free, my face dissolves into another—a much younger face of forty years ago. I am nine years old. It's three o'clock in the afternoon and I have just come home after a miserable day at my new school. A kid bashed into me in the hall, knocking my books out of my hand. As I knelt to pick them up, I heard him snarl the word as he walked away. Later, sitting with my mother in our kitchen, fighting tears, I tell her what happened. She holds me tight to her, rubs my back, and whispers, "Trouble doesn't last always."

The face in the mirror returns to my face of today. I'm no longer nine years old, but my mother's words remain, echoing inside my head. A brief smile appears below my weary eyes.

No, trouble doesn't last always.

★

It's still early in the day when I pull out my phone to call my mom. I had thought to call her hours ago, but I didn't want to alarm her. We all know what a late-night call can mean. In any culture, but especially in the African American culture, when you get a call late at night, you know something terrible has happened. I know that my mother has been watching the events in Ferguson on TV and worrying about me, and yet she has given me the time and space I need without getting on my case to call her more often. I have called her a couple of times in the past week, just to check in, but now I have something I need to tell her.

"Hey," I say when she answers the phone.

"Are you okay?"

"I'm fine." I hear her breath come softly. I realize that from the second she picked up the phone and heard my voice, she has been holding her breath, anticipating bad news.

"I just want to reassure you," I say. "Things have changed. They're happening for the better now. The storm has started to pass. I can feel it."

"Uh-huh," she says, quietly encouraging me, knowing I have more to say.

"I have been out there, walking, and you know—" I feel myself smile. "And, well, people have been asking me why I am the way I am. They want to know where I got this training from."

"Training? What did you say?"

"I said 'I don't know' . . . but I *do* know. And I just want to thank you for raising me the way you did—to be the man that I've become. If Dad were here, I would tell him too. So . . . thank you."

My mother sniffs back a tear and says, "I didn't know of any other way."

"Well, I just hope I've done as well with my kids."

"Oh, you have," my mother says.

★

Please, God—please don't let there be blood on my hands.

A criminal in the crowd threatened to kill a police officer.

A civilian was shot on the street by an unknown gunman.

But no one has died.

"My fear . . . ?" I say to Lori over breakfast. "I didn't want anyone to die. For all the reasons. For every reason. I did not want to be responsible for anyone losing his or her life. I know that if a police officer should die, I'd lose my command. But what would be even worse . . . ?"

Lori waits for me to finish. She knows I'm getting in touch with something I haven't wanted to face.

"I wouldn't be welcome at the funeral," I say.

★

As I stand at the desk in the kitchen, bunching up the rosary beads before putting them in my pocket, I feel Lori standing behind me.

"It wouldn't be your fault," she says.

I turn to her. "It would be my responsibility."

"But—"

"I'm the guy in charge. It would always come back to me."

Lori starts to speak, then stops and lowers her head.

"I can't help it," I say. "That's how I feel. I am responsible for every person in my command, for every person out there."

She nods and bites her lip. You can't argue with how someone feels. We both know that. I slip the rosary beads into my pocket, walk over to her, and wrap my arms around her. We hold each other for a long time, and then I head out the door.

It's a tough job being a police officer.

It's also tough being someone who loves a police officer.

☆

The extreme violence, the looting, and the streets filled with protesters in Ferguson after the shooting of Michael Brown comes to an end. There's no dramatic final act. No curtain falls. It simply stops. The mood on the street shifts. The change I felt twenty-four hours ago continues and builds. The tension that enveloped all of us on the street like a dark menacing fog lifts.

I know it may be temporary—future events may cause emotions to boil over again, and new violence may erupt—but I have to live *now*, in this moment. So many times, especially at news conferences, people have asked me, "What is your plan for tomorrow?"

I always answer the same way: "Tomorrow isn't here."

Today is all we have for sure. *Now* is all we know. And for now, the events of the past two weeks are coming to a stop.

I get an early morning phone call from the governor's office. Based on last night's events, during which we made only six arrests, the governor has decided to withdraw the National Guard. He will not make a big announcement or shine a spotlight on the decision. The Guard troops and armored vehicles will simply depart without fanfare. They will evacuate Ferguson and return West Florissant to what I hope will no longer look even remotely like a street under military occupation.

We all crave a return to something resembling calm. We want the businesses in Ferguson to remain open or to reopen; or if they have been burned out or looted, we want them to rebuild. We want our citizens to go back to work. We want our kids to go back to school. We have spent the past thirteen days living in the clutches of negativity. The world now associates Ferguson—a typical, all-American town—with only negative images: Michael Brown's body lying in the street for hours; the looting and burning of buildings and businesses; throngs of people pouring onto the streets, engulfed by smoke bombs and tear gas; people screaming and cursing at the police; the landscape of a battle zone. It's time to replace those images with positive ones—kids walking to school; people shopping; the police interacting peacefully and meaningfully with people in the community. We've seen firsthand that every picture is worth a thousand words. We need to start broadcasting and posting positive pictures. We need to show the world that we have survived, that we will be coming back, and that we have *learned* from this tragedy.

At least, I *hope* we have learned. I pray to God we have learned. We have to. We have no other choice.

On my way to the command post, I take a detour and drive slowly down West Florissant. Something catches my eye and I pull over. Two policemen walking patrol stop—on their own—to talk to a couple of residents. That's all it is: two officers and two other people, talking. *That's* what the world needs to see. That picture.

I don't know if I inspired these officers by walking every day, twice a day. It doesn't matter. But I do know that a week ago, I would not have seen that image. They say that actions speak louder than words—and here's some concrete evidence.

Actions—even a simple conversation on the street between two police officers and two residents—have power.

When I walk into the command post, I sense another change. The energy in the room feels palpably different. I feel a ray of warmth. It pulses through the room, bringing with it a sense of group accomplishment. For the first time in more than a week, I don't feel under attack. I don't feel judged or scrutinized from anyone out on the street or from anyone inside these walls. The feeling is accompanied by a nod, a tip of a cap, a handshake. It means so much. No, it means *everything*.

Riding this wave of good feelings, I want to get out into the community. I'm planning to walk on West Florissant later today, but I sense that I can send an even bigger message if I appear in the daily lives of everyday Ferguson residents. I arrange to visit a local public library where an art teacher, Carrie Pace, has been meeting with students for the past three days—ever since Walnut Grove, the elementary school where she teaches, closed because of the protests.

I heard that Carrie has been walking on the street, holding a handmade sign over her head that reads, "School Closed? Bring Your Students Here." Underneath are the words "Ferguson Public Library." I'm very moved by this young teacher's dedication to teaching and her commitment to her kids. I want to meet her and express my support.

I round up a couple of officers, and the three of us drive to the library. I walk toward the library's front doors and then hold back for a moment.

Every day as I've walked up and down West Florissant, I've asked myself, *Do I have a destination? Or is this an aimless walk? Where am I going?* And every day I've told myself emphatically, over and over, that I am not just walking in circles. I'm not walking in purposeless loops. I am walking *toward something*, toward an end point. I just don't know what it is yet. It has not yet been revealed. But I have faith that it will be.

Now as I approach the front door of the library, I have a strange intuition that my destination may be discovered inside these doors.

The two officers and I walk into the library and are directed to a large meeting room. I'm stunned by what I see. I was told that when Carrie started her makeshift school program on Monday, only about a dozen kids showed up. Now as we walk into the room, we see upward of 160 schoolchildren sitting at tables around the perimeter, or sprawled on the floor. Carrie moves easily from age group to age group—ranging from kindergarten to sixth grade—overseeing the kids making art projects, filling out math worksheets, and reading books. I can't explain it yet, but I know this is it. I've found my destination.

I can never get over the resilience of kids. They inspire me with their ability to live in the moment, to take life as it comes and make the best of it. The kids seem excited to see us: three police officers in uniform—larger than life to some, perhaps; maybe even heroes to a few. The youngest ones may not even know what's been going on, having been shielded from the news and the negativity.

Carrie says they've been expecting us and that the kindergartners have made gifts for us. I walk over to a cluster of kids on the floor. Their exuberance is contagious. One girl shows me a sock puppet she made. Others show me drawings they've made and coloring books they've been working on. I praise their work and continue moving with Carrie from group to group. This is what it's about—these kids. They are so pure, so innocent, so eager to engage, to learn, to *be*. Seeing how Carrie engages with these kids fills my heart and soul with emotion and hope.

Start here, I think. *Start with these kids. Here lies our future.*

I leave the meeting room with gifts—a sock puppet, a coloring book, and a box of crayons. Just before I exit the library, I tell Carrie, "I know these are not ideal conditions. I can see you're pretty much stretched to your limit."

"We adjust," she says. "We'll go back to Walnut Grove when you think it's time."

"We're getting there," I say.

☆

When I ask police officers to walk the streets of Ferguson, I don't want them to stand in lines, creating a kind of wall between themselves and the people. I ask them to walk, to engage, to connect, to talk. I park my car and walk down West Florissant for a little while, talk to a few people, and then check my watch. I have another meeting in the community. I am going to my old high school, Riverview Gardens High, to sit down with members of the student government, other leaders of the school, and the superintendent. I go alone to give them an opportunity to ask me any questions they have and voice any concerns.

I take my seat in a classroom, and as I settle in, I feel a much different vibe than the one I felt earlier in the library. The students welcome me, but they're wary at the same time. I haven't come to lecture them or state my case—or any case. I've come to ask these young people questions and to listen carefully to their answers. I have no agenda. I've just come to hear them.

I begin with a simple question: "So, how do you feel right now?"

"About the *police*?" a young woman asks. A hair-trigger response.

"Yes."

She hesitates, squirms in her seat, and shares a look with a couple of the other members of the student council. "Honestly? We don't trust the police."

The other students murmur agreement.

"Why don't you trust us?" I ask.

"We're afraid of you," a young man says.

"Why?" I ask the room.

"We feel that you think you're above the law," the first young woman says, to more encouragement, more agreement.

"You act like you can do basically anything you want— *anything*—and get away with it, because you wear that uniform," another young woman says, folding her arms.

The discussion heats up from there. The young people talk over each other, often finishing each other's sentences. I don't judge anything they say. I don't defend myself or the police in general. These students deserve to have this forum to speak their minds freely. I sit among them, allowing them to spew out their anger, confusion, and concerns. It's okay that they become upset. They need a constructive outlet for that anger. I hear their pain and obvious frustration. I take in every word. Then a young woman who hasn't spoken yet starts to say something. The room goes quiet. Her voice raw with anguish, she speaks in a tiny, quivering voice.

"What do you expect?"

I nod, encouraging her to explain, to continue.

"Why do you think we have these negative feelings toward the police, especially now, especially during these days?"

She pauses, allowing her question to sink in, or perhaps to

catch her breath. The room is stone silent, except for the rustle of bodies shifting in chairs.

"I think about those parents," the young woman says finally, her voice scratchy, barely above a whisper. "I think about how *I* would feel if I lost *my* son—a son who was about my age. A young man who could be sitting right here in this room."

"Why did he have to die?" a young man says, his tears flowing. "Maybe he did do something wrong. I don't know. But why did the police have to *kill* him?" The young man looks up and meets my eyes. "Why, Captain Johnson?"

"I don't have the answer," I say, feeling my eyes tearing up. "But maybe if we all ask each other that question together, we can find the answer together."

I look around the room. Several of the kids avoid my eyes. I sigh and then say, "Okay. I'm not asking you to trust us. I'm just asking that you talk to us."

"Same for you," the first young woman says. "Same thing for you."

"Talk," the young man says. "Talk first."

☆

After a very full day, a quiet night follows. Considering the intensity of the last thirteen days, it's an *extremely* quiet night.

At 1:05 a.m., about an hour earlier than usual, I convene my end-of-the-day press conference. Around midnight, I asked a couple of officers at the command post to bring out the same table we used several nights ago to display the guns and the Molotov cocktail. Tonight, again, the table is covered with a lumpy plastic tarp.

I trudge toward the assembled media and pause in front of

the flashing cameras and video recorders. My legs feel leaden. I don't know when I have ever felt so physically tired, and yet tonight I feel emotionally stronger than at any other time during these two weeks in Ferguson. I have a lot to say tonight, and I have written much of it down. I want to make sure I get it right. Tonight, I wear my glasses.

I wait for the media to settle in. As usual, they spread out before me in a haphazard semicircle, with several people sitting on the ground. I pause before I begin, briefly scanning the strip mall that has housed our command post and makeshift media bullpen. So many of these people have spent as much time as I have here, devoting hours upon hours and enduring sleepless nights, dedicating themselves to getting the story—and in most cases getting the story *right*. I appreciate their hard work and dedication more than they know. They are a necessary part of what has happened here.

I lower my head and begin to read my statement. I immediately hear the urgency in my voice, an urgency tinged with excitement. Though I can't say it out loud, I almost want to shout that I have arrived at my destination.

"We had to respond to fewer incidents tonight," I read. "There were no Molotov cocktails tonight. No fires. No shootings. We did not see a single handgun. And again tonight, for the second night in a row, we did not deploy smoke devices . . . no tear gas and no mace. And *again* tonight"—I enunciate each word precisely—"no police officer fired a single shot."

I hear nothing. Not a sound. I look up to make sure the members of the media are following me, that they are listening. I scan the cluster of people in front of me and see only rapt faces. They sense it. They sense the change.

I look back at the page in my hand and pick up where I left off.

"Tuesday night, the number of arrests was forty-seven. Last night, the number of arrests was six. And tonight, as of 12:30 a.m., there have been seven arrests."

I look up again to make sure everyone is hearing this.

"Three of the seven were from Detroit. Four were from the St. Louis area. Five were failure to disperse, one was for an existing warrant, and one was for driving through a checkpoint."

I fold the paper and look out at the media. I speak now extemporaneously—no notes, nothing planned, not thinking at all about what I am about to say.

"I mentioned that there were some good things going on in the community today. I'd heard that teachers and volunteers were using the Ferguson Public Library as an education center for children who still aren't in school because of what's going on here in this city. Monday was the first day of the program called School for Peace. It was organized by Carrie Pace, a teacher at Walnut Grove School. Monday, there were twelve children in the program. Today that number had grown to more than 160 children. I visited the facility with some other police officers earlier this afternoon. I can tell you it is a beautiful environment."

I pause and swallow. I clear my throat. I don't want to lose it—not yet.

"I want to show you something."

The media members in front of me rustle; a few start jockeying gently for position, edging forward to get a better view.

"Remember the other night when some of you doubted that agitators had fired handguns and thrown Molotov cocktails at police? To prove it I showed you the guns and a Molotov cocktail."

I hear a few murmurs in response.

"I want to show you now that things have changed. I want to show you that we have come to a new place."

I nod at the police officer to my left. He removes the tarp.

On the table are the sock puppet, the coloring book, and the box of crayons.

With a catch in my throat, I say, "It's time for our community to go back to work. It's time for our kids to go back to school."

I hear sounds now that I can't quite place. I remove my glasses, wipe my eyes, and look out at the members of the media. I identify the sounds now. Several reporters are sobbing. I nod and tilt my head at the sock puppet on the table.

"We may never come to an end. We have to *try*, and keep trying, but that end may be a very long way off. We may not get there. I know that. But we have to *try*. So tonight I say, '*Enough.*' Tomorrow we start a new beginning."

EPILOGUE

AFTER FERGUSON

The story of Ferguson remains the story of America.

WESLEY LOWERY
THEY CAN'T KILL US ALL

AFTER THOSE THIRTEEN DAYS, calm comes to Ferguson in fits and starts. The crowds on West Florissant thin, hour by hour, day by day, and finally the protests fizzle out.

I continue to walk, but I start spending more days speaking to community organizations and driving to businesses that are rebuilding. Governor Nixon never officially relieves me of my duty as head of security. There is no formal handoff, but local police take over daily law enforcement. At the same time, the Department of Justice commissions what they promise will be a thorough and comprehensive study of systemic racism within the Ferguson Police Department. St. Louis County Police Chief Jon Belmar still works next to me with complete commitment. We don't always agree, but if, God forbid, I ever find myself facing another "Ferguson," I would want Jon right by my side. A day or two after the protests diminish, I have a meeting with Jon, and I simply tell him, "Thank you." We clasp hands and hug.

On Monday, August 25, I leave to attend Michael Brown's funeral, held at Friendly Temple Missionary Baptist Church in St. Louis, not far from the house I lived in when I was in early elementary school. More than twenty-five hundred people pack the sanctuary, and another two thousand spill outside onto the church grounds. I drive to the service with another officer, and we park up the street from the church. As I approach the building, people start to recognize me and point me out, and soon camera crews from local news stations rush over to me. I hold up my hand and say quietly, "I'm sorry, but out of respect to the family, I won't be doing any interviews or talking to the media today."

I wend my way toward the front doors of the church, peer inside, take a couple of steps in, and suddenly freeze. I feel it then, a kind of wind rising and floating from the depths of the sanctuary near Michael Brown's coffin—a wind of raw pain. This pain has its own life, its own breath. This pain—this wrenching, stabbing pain—comes when you grieve over an unexpected death, a death that has come too soon. I lived that pain when my brother died.

This day, in this sanctuary, I live it again. The pain blows toward me and staggers me. My hands start to tremble and my heart races. I feel myself backing away and out the door. Before I realize what I'm doing or where I'm going, my legs have carried me off the church grounds, and I'm walking up the street, back to the car. I get into the backseat, my heart pounding, my head lowered. I stay transfixed in that position for the rest of the funeral. I tell myself that I've come back to the car because I don't want to be a distraction—partly true—but mostly I feel devastated by the sheer pain, a pain so raw, so real, and so potent that I feel it here, sitting in the car, a block away from the funeral.

☆

In late September, some people construct a memorial to Michael Brown on Canfield Drive, where he lived and died. One morning, residents find the memorial destroyed, trampled, burned to the ground. A group gathers at the site and rebuilds the memorial. That evening, protesters gather outside the Ferguson police station, calling for Chief Tom Jackson to resign. After a while Chief Jackson appears, buffered by fifty police officers, and tries to explain that changes will be made in the Ferguson Police Department. This vague response only agitates the protesters. People throw bottles and rocks. The police sweep into the crowd and arrest eight people.

A few nights later, protesters and clergy once again convene outside the police station. The police announce through bullhorns that people will be arrested if they don't clear the street. Ignoring this warning, several clergy members begin praying in the police parking lot. The police make another announcement— that they will round people up if they don't stop chanting and praying by 11:00 p.m.

I get a call to come down to the police station, my first call to Ferguson in a month. I arrive to find protesters and police facing off in the parking lot. The sight feels eerily familiar and chokingly sad. The police announce that they have invoked the "five-second rule," meaning protesters have five seconds to disperse before police will arrest them. At that point, we hear gunshots, and both police and protesters retreat. Sensing that a storm of violence is approaching again, I grab a bullhorn. I tell the crowd that we will not enforce the five-second rule as long as they protest peacefully. The crowd cheers, but I hear some police officers behind me groaning, complaining, cursing. I no longer care what they think. I only care about doing what I think is right.

We came to an end, I tell myself in an effort to keep my spirits up, *but things have not stopped.*

★

We slog our way through an unseasonably warm October, with people protesting sporadically and without violence. I still make it a point when I can to walk the streets, talk to residents, and continue community outreach, speaking at schools and at local civic and youth groups. At the same time, I'm aware that the city of Ferguson has begun a nervous waiting game anticipating the grand jury's decision on Darren Wilson, the officer who shot Michael Brown.

In late November, three and a half months after Michael Brown's death and those thirteen days of protest, a crowd of a few hundred people gathers at the Ferguson police station, awaiting news of the grand jury's verdict. As the minutes pass, the people grow angrier and more restless. People shout and begin chanting, "We want a timetable for justice!"

Across town, on West Florissant, business owners have boarded up their stores with sheets of plywood, gearing up for a possible resurgence of violence and looting. Many have scrawled "We're Open" in red and black marker across the face of the wood. As the community awaits the decision, their anger simmers with each passing minute.

When the announcement comes that the grand jury has

decided not to indict Darren Wilson, the crowd in front of the police station goes insane. They pelt the building with whatever objects they have at hand. On West Florissant, groups of people descend on the businesses near Canfield Drive—and with camera crews following and filming every move, they attack the McDonald's. When they discover that the windows are impenetrable, impossible to smash, they swarm next door to Ferguson Market & Liquor, where Michael Brown had swiped the cigarillos. Someone smashes the front window with a baseball bat, and a stream of people rush inside. Minutes later, the looters begin torching every business they can. The police response is uncertain, delayed. The rioters have their way.

"See, the police don't care," someone shouts in the middle of the mayhem. "They just stand there. They don't care if we burn black businesses."

The next day, Chief Jon Belmar shockingly admits in an interview, "We didn't expect a response of this magnitude. We really didn't."

In fact, the immediate reaction after the grand jury verdict is more intense than most nights after Michael Brown's death. Governor Jay Nixon declares a state of emergency and sends in the National Guard. As protesters and rioters once again take to the streets of Ferguson, protests break out in more than one hundred cities across America.

I don't know exactly what to expect, or to what magnitude, but I'm not at all surprised by the visceral and violent reaction. We have experienced a few months of relative calm, but as I walk through the neighborhood and talk to the people, I know we have a long way to go. The grand jury's decision leaves a rancid taste in people's mouths.

★

After a couple of days of protests, tensions cool down. Calm is once again restored to Ferguson, and the year ends quietly.

To my surprise, in February 2015 I receive an award from a local church. Ever since the events in Ferguson, I have embraced my faith more strongly than ever before. I feel immensely humbled and grateful to receive this honor.

As I stand on the stage in the church sanctuary, I face a standing room–only crowd. The chairwoman of the committee that chose me for the award begins to speak.

"First of all, I want to thank God for sending us this great man, Captain Johnson, at a time when we really needed him most." She looks at me, her lip trembling, and says, "Thank you very much."

After she reads the inscription on the plaque, she hands the microphone to a young pastor who is standing at my side. He nods at me, turns to the congregants, and says, "You know the Bible says greater love is nothing less than this—that he or she is willing to lay down his or her life . . . for *friends*. And when you stand up in the midst of a turbulent situation like the one the captain stood up in, you don't know what's going to happen. But it takes the courage that only God can give, and it takes an anointing on your life to say, 'I want to be an instrument in the hands of God.'"

With his eyes welling up, the pastor looks at me and then focuses again on the congregation.

"This brother has given us an example of how to live our lives. Martin Luther King said that those who have not found something worth dying for are not fit to live. This brother has found a cause worth dying for. Let's get behind him and lift him up with *prayer power*, knowing that God can do exceedingly, abundantly, and above what we can ask or imagine. God bless you, my brother, and keep up the mighty work that you do through God."

I thank him, take the microphone, and look out into the congregation. Since the events of Ferguson, everything in my life has gone through intense change. Some of these changes I'm aware of, and some I can only sense. I have questioned God, especially after the deaths of my grandfather Sherman and my brother, and after my father's accident and his later death from Alzheimer's. But during those days in Ferguson, I embraced my faith, relied on my faith, and really found my faith. My faith has brought me power. My faith has brought me peace. And now, standing here, the acknowledgment of my faith gushes from me: "To my Lord, God, my Savior, I give thanks. To this pastor, I appreciate you very much."

I pause, briefly close my eyes, and allow the words to come— a message I have not prepared, but that I know will flow. At times like these, I rely on my faith for the words to come. I definitely feel that I am an instrument in the hands of God.

I open my eyes, blink, and say, "I can tell you that in the midst of the storm, you can't see your way. And that's where I was in Ferguson. I got down on my knees and asked God, 'What can I do? What should I do?' When I got up, the prayers came in. I would walk the streets of Ferguson and see people just like you, and they would say, 'Can we pray for you?' They would touch me. They would touch my arms, and my shoulders, and my head, and they would pray for me. *That's* where my courage came from."

The congregation starts to applaud.

"It's not that I'm a better man than anyone else. It's *faith*. And trust in him who will lead us. I know we'll be better. We have to be. We're going to move forward. And I'm going to be here."

I look over at the pastor and smile. "There's that song where the mother gets into the closet—"

The congregation applauds again, and several people shout. One voice breaks above the rest, hollering, "Go ahead, Captain, tell it!"

I wait for the congregation to settle, and then I say, "In that command post in Ferguson, there was a little bathroom. That became my closet. I would go in there, and sometimes I would cry and I would pray. I would pray and I would cry. When I came out"—I drop my voice. I feel the tears pouring down my cheeks—"I had the strength of God with me."

The applause thunders around me. I sniff, pull myself together, and say, "This community is going to be better. We just have to all lift our heads up. Thank you once again for this honor."

⭐

On March 4, 2015, the Department of Justice concludes an extensive six-month investigation that, according to the *New York Times*, finds the Ferguson Police Department "was routinely violating the constitutional rights of its black residents."[1] According to the *Times*, the report "describes a city where the police used force almost exclusively on blacks and regularly stopped people without probable cause. Racial bias is so ingrained . . . that Ferguson officials circulated racist jokes on their government email accounts."[2] The article goes on to say that "those findings reinforce what the city's black residents have been saying publicly since the shooting in August, that the criminal justice system in Ferguson works differently for blacks and whites."

I think about the group of young men that Don Lemon and I spoke to during those days in Ferguson, who talked about being targeted by police just because they were black. I think about the students I spoke to at Riverview Gardens High, my old high school, who told me how they feared the police, how they believed the police thought they were above the law. I read the article in the newspaper again and see that the investigation conducted hundreds of interviews and looked at thirty-five thousand pages of police reports.

The report's conclusions take my breath away.

On March 11, 2015, one week after the Department of Justice report comes out, Ferguson Police Chief Tom Jackson resigns. His resignation sparks a rally outside the police station. Many of the people assemble peacefully, but others, perhaps enraged at learning that Chief Jackson will receive a full-year's salary and benefits, scream and taunt the police, other protesters, and the media.

☆

When the DOJ report comes out, I take some heat. I absorb criticism for not spending enough time at the command post and for spending too much time talking with the media. Critics pile on, saying there didn't seem to be any "direction" and that I didn't completely follow the prescribed guidelines.

"We should rebut this," a colonel in the Patrol says to me.

"Does it matter?" I ask. "I stand by what I did."

Thankfully, we can say that after Michael Brown's death, we had no other fatalities. And overall, Ferguson experienced minor property damage—at least compared to the devastation years ago in Watts and Detroit, and in South Central Los Angeles after the Rodney King beating.

As far as the NIMS guidelines, I hadn't seen any that really applied to Ferguson, that mentioned empathy or connecting with the community or listening—really listening—to what people were desperately trying to say.

I saw no mention of humanity. Or heart.

Those were the strategies I used.

I know police tactics. I know how to fight. Those tactics did not apply. Maybe I did break the rules. But maybe we need new rules, new guidelines.

I make no excuses.

I have no regrets.

I'm not going to debate or defend what I did.

But if—God forbid—we ever find ourselves facing another Ferguson, I would do exactly the same thing: I would go out on the street, and I would walk.

☆

Baltimore. New York. Cleveland. Dallas. Minneapolis. Memphis. Cincinnati.

It doesn't end.

It doesn't stop.

Every news report from every city mentions Ferguson, compares that city to Ferguson. Every city *becomes* Ferguson. Ferguson becomes more than a place. Sadly, Ferguson becomes a condition.

I hear talk about remaking the Ferguson Police Department and retraining police in general. I hear discussions about issuing body cameras to every police officer on patrol. Someone asks me how I feel about that idea.

"That's all fine," I say. "But we have to do more. We have to retrain ourselves as human beings."

I believe that, with all my heart.

We need to change the core of who we are. We need to change people's points of view. We have to alter our behavior. And we have to start this training when people are young, when they are children. Children don't come into the world with biases. When I say *baby steps*, we need to put the emphasis on both words.

See people as people.

Start there.

Abandon labels.

Try not to prejudge—no matter what you may think of people by their appearance.

Early in my career, I arrested a guy and took him in to fill out the appropriate paperwork. Going through the forms, I arrived at a question that asked if there were any identifying tattoos. I felt dumb asking that question because I could see he had a tattoo on his back, snaking up his neck from beneath his shirt.

"No," the man said, squirming in his chair. "No tattoos."

I started to laugh. "Hey, I can see you have a tattoo."

"Oh. Okay. Yeah."

"Well, what is it?"

He hesitated and then pulled down his shirt to show me. I couldn't see the entire tattoo, but I clearly saw the letters *KKK*.

"Look," he said, his face reddening as he struggled to explain, "I know what you're thinking—"

"It's okay," I said.

"What?"

"It's all right. You don't have to explain."

He looked confused as I went on to the next question. We

continued filling out the forms, and as we did, we began talking casually, one person to another. When I finished the intake procedure, the man looked at me earnestly.

"Listen, about my tattoo—"

He stopped as once again he searched to find the right words. Finally, he took a deep breath, exhaled, and said, "Thank you for not judging me. Thank you for treating me like a person."

☆

I'm asked to speak to police officers in training. Standing in front of a group of trainees in a classroom, I share a story from Ferguson.

"During one of the days of chaos, I spot a trooper leading a man he's arrested for disorderly conduct and failing to disperse. The trooper has the man's hands handcuffed behind his back. The man's young son follows them both and begins to imitate his dad. The young boy sticks his hands behind his back and pretends that he, too, has been handcuffed."

I pause to allow this image to sink in.

"I walk over to the trooper and tell him to take the handcuffs off the man and let him go. He hesitates. I can see he's upset with me, but I outrank him. After a few seconds, he takes off the guy's cuffs and joins another trooper watching us on the sidewalk. The guy who was arrested stands off to the side, rubbing his wrists. I go over to him, pull him a few feet away, and say to him, quietly, 'Is this what you want to teach your son? Is this what you want him to see? He's modeling his dad. He wants to be like *you*. He shouldn't be out here. Take him home.'"

I pause to gauge the response of the officers in the room. Half the trainees look appalled; the other half look confused.

"I walk over to the trooper who made the arrest and the other trooper he's standing with. I could see they were upset with me for letting the guy go. 'I know you guys don't agree with me,' I say. They don't respond, but they don't have to. They're obviously angry. And then I ask, 'Do you guys have sons?'"

The officers in training rustle in their seats. They didn't expect me to ask the troopers this question.

"The troopers tell me they both have sons. I say to them, my eyes going from one to the other, 'When you go home tonight, I want you to look at your sons and ask yourselves if you would want them to see you the way this young boy was seeing his dad.' And then I say, 'When you guys come back to work tomorrow, if you disagree with what I've done, I want you to go to my boss and tell him. Tell him how you feel.'"

I begin hearing another sound in the room—the sound of choked-back tears.

"The next morning I come into work, and I see those troopers. They come up to me, both of them, and they say, 'I understand. Thank you.'"

We rarely learn from lectures.

We learn from our stories.

We are our stories.

★

August 2015.

One year after Michael Brown was killed, here's what I hear:

"*We don't trust the police.*"

"*We need the police.*"

Two separate screams.

I see Michael Brown's mother at an event honoring mothers

who've lost sons to violence. I see her interact with some of the other mothers.

The loss of a child. The loss of a son. As members of an exclusive and terrible club, these women share a pain both unfathomable and unbearable. The pain rips a piece of their soul.

When I have the opportunity, I approach Michael Brown's mother. We talk quietly and warmly, and then we hug. As we do, I feel that she—and Ferguson itself—has at least taken a small step toward some form of healing.

I also meet with Michael Brown's father. He, too, has started to come out into the community. When we talk, I don't expect too much—I can't expect anything—but I feel that with him, too, healing has begun.

Tiny steps.

Inch by inch . . .

On the Saturday of the one-year anniversary, a large group of people walk to the high school that Michael Brown attended. I join the march. Over and over people say to me, "I want to believe we're moving forward. I *want* to believe that."

Wanting to believe. I think that even *wanting to believe* means we have moved forward. That itself is a type of action. A type of faith.

The Highway Patrol has assigned some troopers to be part of this parade, along with officers from the St. Louis County Police Department. We drive along the route in John Deere Gators, passing out bottles of water and Popsicles to the marchers. The crushing Missouri heat punishes the parade marchers, but the water and Popsicles give everyone a boost.

"You can do it," I shout to a couple of marchers who have slowed down and are beginning to fade.

"How about a ride?" one of them says to the trooper riding next to me. The trooper laughs and reaches out his hand.

A year ago, this trooper may have been standing on this same street wearing riot gear. Instead of Gators, we saw armored vehicles; burning buildings; SWAT; smoke bombs; tear gas.

I'm not saying we've come far.

But we have come somewhere.

Baby steps.

Inches.

☆

In the years since I bore responsibility for security in Ferguson, I've thought a lot about the importance of media. The media bear the responsibility to report what happens to people in this country, to show the truth. During the events in Ferguson, we in law enforcement didn't always trust the media. Frankly, police in urban settings often hesitate to cooperate fully with the media because we're afraid we'll be shown in a bad light. Now that everyone has a phone with a camera, some police have reason to be nervous.

We still need to do a better job of integrating police into our communities. It's the only way out of this. Policing is personal. It has to be. The police need to go into those neighborhoods where we might find ourselves unwelcome. We have to get past those barriers and devote ourselves to being involved in the community. We need to get to know the people we serve and protect. We have to police poor communities the same way we police rich communities. The police need to be present, engaged, and seen.

I still walk. I still make myself present. I shake hands; I ask people about their day; I hug people.

I walk over to one guy and I start to hug him.

"Hey, I'm dirty. I just got off work," he says, laughing.

"It doesn't matter. I'm gonna hug you anyway."

And I do.

⭐

I pray differently now.

I don't ask.

I simply give thanks—for Lori and my kids, for my mom and my sister, and for all the people in my life. I give thanks for the strength to pick myself up when I fall, and for the faith that powers my life.

I visit my dad and Bernard at the cemetery, and I give thanks to them. I thank them for all they've given me. I thank them for everything.

And I thank God for giving me the strength to face tomorrow.

We have a long way to go, I know that, but I believe in tomorrow.

That's what I believe in most of all.

Tomorrow.

A new day.

Another chance.

⭐

I speak to a group of students at Lipscomb University in Nashville. I speak intimately about my faith. The three days I spend with these students move me deeply. I learn much more than I teach.

"Sometimes we shy away from talking about our faith in public, or even with our friends," I say. "I can tell you, I used to be one of those guys. And then Ferguson happened. Those days allowed me to reach deep inside me and find a depth of faith I never knew I had."

I pause and scan the faces of the students looking raptly at me. The only sound I hear is the pulse of my own heart.

"We had briefings before we started our day," I say, my voice dipping just above a hush. "The first day I took over, I told all the police officers gathered there that we were going to pray. A chaplain started the prayer, and I could see that some of the policemen didn't close their eyes. I heard mumbling. Grumbling. I heard someone say, 'This guy can't make me pray.' And I heard worse."

I smile, remembering, envisioning the faces of some of those policemen.

"As the days went on, something happened during that morning prayer. More and more police officers closed their eyes—until finally one day I saw that every eye was closed, every police officer praying. And then I saw tears coming down their faces."

Before me, some of the students begin to cry.

Faith, it seems, is infectious.

★

I began with a story of being guilty of bias. I end with a story of being a victim of bias.

One Friday night, Lori and I splurged and went out to a fancy restaurant. After dinner, I took a different route home.

"Where are you going?" Lori asked.

"I decided tomorrow's the day I get started on those house projects I promised you," I said. "I want to see what time the hardware store opens in the morning."

I drove into the hardware store's parking lot, slowed the car in front of the store, and peered at the store's hours printed on the door. When I had the information I needed, I drove slowly out of the parking lot.

As soon as we reached the street, a police car rolled up behind us and flashed its lights. I pulled over. I heard the thump of the police officer's boots on the pavement before I actually saw him. I lowered my window and smiled at the officer. Big guy. Strapping. All business. White.

"Good evening, officer."

"Good evening." He eyed me and Lori, then scanned the inside of the car, training his eyes on the back seat. He looked back at me—I was wearing a suit and tie and Lori was in an evening dress.

"I'm wondering why you pulled into that parking lot," he said.

I tried not to laugh.

Here we have two people north of forty years old, dressed up for the evening, driving in a freshly washed, late-model car, with no sign of burglary tools or ski masks in the backseat, and I have to wonder, *Does he think we were casing the hardware store? Really?*

Then, as if he were reading my mind or trying to justify why he pulled us over, he said, "We've had some thefts in the area."

Now I did laugh.

"Officer, we're coming from dinner. This is my wife. I was checking to see what time the store opened—"

Still all business, still eyeing us with what I sense is a trace of suspicion, he won't let it go.

"This store has been broken into several times."

Now, I know he didn't pull us over because we're black.

I do believe that.

But once you saw we were black, you thought we were casing the store, didn't you?

I don't say that.

I don't want to believe that.

After he saw how we were dressed, how we behaved, and heard why we pulled in front of the hardware store, he should have acted differently. He should have realized we weren't thieves. He might have apologized. We might have shared a laugh.

Would he have acted differently if we were white?

James Baldwin said, "Not everything that is faced can be changed; but nothing can be changed until it is faced."[4]

We all have to face our biases.

Only then will things change.

★

August 2017.

Hope will arise—from our pain, from our distrust, from our sorrow, from our ashes.

On the site of the former QuikTrip, the Urban League of Metropolitan St. Louis and the town of Ferguson built a gleaming new youth center, the Ferguson Community Empowerment Center. Its purpose is to provide job training and placement services.

I attend the dedication ceremony, along with hundreds of others. As I walk into the building, I see a bench with a plaque in memory of Michael Brown and pause to read the inscription. Inside the foyer, a collage of photographs covers an entire wall. Riveted, I follow the photos upward, and there I see . . . myself.

In uniform.

Peering off slightly, my jaw clenched in determination.

I could interpret the look on my face in many ways: I could be looking at a crowd of protesters. I could be taking a moment to pray. I could be talking to my dad.

I stare into my own eyes and realize that I will live here forever, part of the fabric of this community; a fixture of its past, present, and future.

Today, Ferguson lives within me, a breathing piece of my heart. An attitude. A part of who I am. Part of my definition.

I don't walk as much now. West Florissant is not by nature a walking street. So I drive. But I remain present. I get out of my car and I speak to residents. I interact. I acknowledge people's continuing struggles and concerns. Most of all, I try to listen.

As I wait at a stoplight one day, a young man on a bicycle leads his two kids on their bikes across the street. I roll down my window and call to the young dad.

"Hey."

The young man stops.

I smile at him. "I just want to say that I like seeing this. I'm proud of you. You're a good dad."

"Thank you," he says. "You made my day."

"You made mine," I say.

This is what Ferguson has become to me. This is what Ferguson has taught me. This is what Ferguson has done for me. This is what Ferguson insists that we all need to do, every single one of us.

We have to reach out.

Talking. Listening. Hearing. Hugging. And understanding.

We have to reach out to each other.

I ask myself, "What are you reaching *for*?"

I don't know exactly.

I look at my hands and see that they are empty.

Even after going through those thirteen days in Ferguson—thirteen days of chaos and success and failure and pain and struggle, and then, finally, a semblance of calm—my hands are still empty.

People ask me, "What will you do now?"

I ask myself, *What* should *I do now?*

What should we all do?

We have to keep reaching.

That's what I know.

That's what I will do.

I will keep reaching.

We have to keep reaching—until our hands are no longer empty . . . until we can hold on to each other.

NOTES

DAY 6 (DAYLIGHT): A DIFFERENT MORNING
1. "Gov. [Jay] Nixon's News Conference on Ferguson," CNN, transcript of press conference at University of Missouri–St. Louis, August 14, 2014, www.cnn.com /TRANSCRIPTS/1408/14/cg.01.html; "Missouri Governor Jay Nixon Ferguson Press Conference (C-SPAN)," YouTube video, 1:35, from press conference aired August 14, 2014, posted by C-SPAN, August 14, 2014, www.youtube.com/watch?v =dTIeRVIWIyk.
2. "Gov. Nixon: Highway Patrol to Take Over Protest Response," CNN, transcript of press conference at University of Missouri–St. Louis, August 14, 2014; http:// transcripts.cnn.com/TRANSCRIPTS/1408/14/cg.02.html. Italics added for inflection.

DAY 7: "SAVE OUR SONS"
1. "Ferguson police release the name of officer involved in Michael Brown shooting," YouTube video of press conference aired August 15, 2014, posted by *PBS NewsHour*, August 15, 2014, www.youtube.com/watch?v=6XJ1Kh1CTB8.
2. Captain Ronald Johnson, "Ferguson, Missouri, Police Shooting and Protests," C-SPAN video of press conference aired August 15, 2014, https://www.c-span.org /video/?321034-1/news-conference-ferguson-missouri-shooting.

DAY 8: "NO MORE THAN I CAN BEAR"
1. "FULL Governor Nixon press conference (About Ferguson and Mike Brown)," YouTube video of press conference aired August 16, 2014, posted by Trayvon George, August 16, 2014, https://www.youtube.com/watch?v=keRCkWdN4Lg.

DAY 9: "I AM YOU"
1. "Captain Ron Johnson addresses Michael Brown rally at Greater Grace Church," YouTube video, posted by Egberto Willies, August 17, 2014, www.youtube.com /watch?v=4-wkpbFU_d4.

2. "Capt. Johnson: 'We had to act,'" MSNBC video of press conference aired August 18, 2014, http://www.msnbc.com/the-cycle/watch/capt.-johnson-we-had -to-act-319015492000.

DAY 10: A BULLET HAS NO NAME
1. "Police Press Conference in Ferguson," Facing History and Ourselves, transcript of press conference on August 19, 2014, accessed March 13, 2018, https://www .facinghistory.org/resource-library/facing-ferguson-news-literacy-digital-age /police-press-conference-ferguson.
2. Ibid.
3. Ibid.
4. Ibid.

EPILOGUE: AFTER FERGUSON
1. Matt Apuzzo, "Ferguson Police Routinely Violate Rights of Blacks, Justice Dept. Finds," *New York Times*, March 3, 2015; www.nytimes.com/2015/03/04/us/justice -department-finds-pattern-of-police-bias-and-excessive-force-in-ferguson.html.
2. Ibid.
3. Ibid.
4. James Baldwin, "As Much Truth as One Can Bear," *New York Times Book Review*, January 14, 1962, republished in *The Cross of Redemption: Uncollected Writings*, Randall Kenan, ed. (New York: Vintage International, 2011), 42.

ACKNOWLEDGMENTS

RON

First, I am grateful to Eric Rhone Sr., my agent and friend, for his insistence that I "step onto the path" of this journey.

I also must thank Anthony Mattero for steering us to Tyndale Momentum, not just our publisher but also our home. I thank everyone there, in every capacity, with special gratitude to Carol Traver, who saw the value of my journey and continues to be our most enthusiastic supporter; Dave Lindstedt for his careful editing; and Dean Renninger for his beautiful and moving cover design.

In many ways, our lives are shaped by the individuals we meet along the way. My initial relationship with my coauthor, Alan Eisenstock, could be defined as strictly business, with Alan very businesslike on the specifics of his craft, describing to me step-by-step the process of authoring a book. And then we began.

Day 1: Alan and I are scheduled to start our journey together, but our conversation never leads us to *step onto the path*. Instead, we talk about our lives. More importantly, we talk about our faith—I'm a Baptist and Alan is Jewish. At the outset, we are two strangers of different faiths crossing paths. By the time we *step onto the path* together on Day 2, we are brothers on a journey that will eventually produce *13 Days in Ferguson*.

Alan, you have confirmed my belief that when individuals open themselves up to each other, they discover how much more alike they are than different. I have been privileged and blessed to have you help me *step onto the path*, providing strength during a deeply emotional journey.

Lindsay Lyle Ripley, your courage and determination have touched my soul. I have learned from you that we must always keep running toward our dreams and never stop reaching. Your parents, James Paul Ripley and Mary Kathleen Kearney Ripley, and your sister, Claire Elizabeth Ripley, inspire me every day with their courage.

Growing up, all a son wants is to walk with the same strength as his hero. When age and health slowed my hero's walk, this son began to see the faith in the slow walk that allowed his hero to confront Alzheimer's with courage. At times, it hurt unspeakably when my hero could not remember things about his son. But the son learned to see the grace in his hero while never forgetting his God. I am grateful to my father, Roscoe Johnson, for displaying strength and faith even when the path ahead was unknown.

A mother of faith required her son to pray before bed and meals because she believed. The son did not always understand why, but he prayed anyway, because it was mandated. The mother continued to pray—and to expect the same of her son—even when he moved away. To my mom, Annie Johnson: How blessed I am for your mandating prayer into my life. Mom, throughout this journey, your daily prayers have comforted me, just as they did when I was a child kneeling in prayer before bedtime.

Growing up with a sister and a brother, I would sometimes say words I didn't mean, just to stop the teasing and squabbling. I sometimes feared that those words would break us apart, but they never did. To my sister, Regina: I am grateful for you. You are my biggest critic and staunchest ally. I could not have walked this path without you with me, my defender.

Two brothers, sharing a room. The older brother wants his own space, his privacy, but the house is too small. In time, the younger brother begins to look up to his older brother, and the older brother begins to accept the living arrangement. Eventually, the older brother leaves home, and his dreams become filled with memories of that shared room. As the younger brother grows up, the older brother admires his strength, his character, and—most of all—his ability to know no strangers. In memory of my brother, Bernard: I am grateful that you taught me not to view other people as strangers but to embrace everyone we encounter as we journey through life.

August 20, 1988: A man marries the love of his life, and two kids are born from that love. The man sees himself as a rock that the family stands on. He believes the rock will never crumble beneath his family. Any crack in the rock is hidden, masked. But the days and nights on the streets of Ferguson in August 2014 cause deeper cracks to emerge in the rock, and the rock can no longer hide them. No longer is he able to fight off a recurring thought: *What will happen to my family?*

To my wife, Lori: I honor you for becoming the rock that I leaned on. In fact, you were the rock on which our *entire* family stood. You assured us all that crumbling was never an option. Thank you, Lori, forever.

When a father's daughter is born, he thanks God for blessing him with an angel. When the father endures some of the toughest days of his life, his angel sends him a Bible verse to encourage him. To my daughter, Amanda: Thank you for the Bible verse you sent me during this journey. It became the light that illumined my path.

A mother holds a father's son, and the father stares into the baby's eyes with a glowing pride. The father has dreams of being a great father and having a certain, specific father-son relationship. As the years go by, life intrudes and things change and the father begins to see the relationship differently. He sees that this child will always be his son, but the son grows to be a man, too, and has his own mind and his own advice to give. The father remains the son's biggest fan, continuing to provide support while always letting the son know how proud he is of him. Bradley, my son, I was honored when I realized that our father-son relationship had changed. You not only became a man but also became my best friend. When you sent me that touching text during the early days of the journey, I knew that no matter what, my best friend would always be there.

A man's father has passed away, but the man still yearns to hear that fatherly voice of support. One day, very early in the morning, he receives a call from his father-in-law—providing that fatherly voice, not as an obligation but as an expression of love. To my father-in-law and fellow brother in blue, Charles McCrary: I needed the wisdom from your call that day more than any other words we have shared during our cherished relationship.

Every morning as the trooper leaves for work, he worries about who will check on his wife when he is unable to call her. Each night when he comes home, his wife tells him of her conversation with the lady who has called each day, like clockwork, while he is on his journey. To my mother-in-law, Jeanie McCrary: Thank you for being Lori's guardian angel during this journey.

To my spiritual leaders, extended family, mentors, friends, and everyone who has crossed my path in life, in Ferguson and throughout the country: Please know that the experiences, lessons, prayers, hugs, and encouragement have all shaped and affected my *steps* along this journey. I thank you from the bottom of my heart.

ALAN

All books are, in some way, miracles. You never know how they will begin and how they will turn out—or, in some cases, whether they will turn into anything at all. Except this one. I never doubted that *13 Days in Ferguson* would turn out the way it did. From the first moment when Ron and I spoke on the phone, I felt a spark that went beyond a mere connection. *I know you*, I thought. *It's as if I've always known you.* Maybe that was the miracle.

Ron, thank you for opening up to me, for trusting me, for showing me Ferguson and the road you walked. Thank you for laughing and crying with me, for challenging me, and for making me look at the world differently—ultimately with greater depth and feeling. Our writing process became a mix of confession and therapy, for both of us. I am very honored and thankful to call you my friend.

Lori, you are a guiding light, a pinnacle of strength, wisdom, enthusiasm, and good cheer. Ron and I could not have done the book without you. Thank you.

We could not have found a better home than Tyndale House. Every person there deserves a mention and a thank-you, but we have to begin with Carol Traver. You are a force—wise, strong, kind, and hilarious.

Thanks for your vision, guidance, insight, openness, directness, and excellent book recommendations. Dave Lindstedt, you are incredibly thorough, and you pushed me hard. I may have resisted a little at first, but your edits were intelligent, true, sharp, and pure. Thank you. Dean Renninger, your overall design—and especially the cover—is a riveting study of deep emotion, a book cover as art. Thank you for your kind words and keen eye.

Eric Rhone Sr., thank you for your savvy, toughness, and good nature, and for always having Ron's back.

Jessica Stahl, thank you.

Anthony Mattero—superstar, superpartner, brother—you're the best.

Thanks to my friends David Ritz, Madeline and Phil Schwarzman, Susan Pomerantz and George Weinberger, Susan Baskin and Richard Gerwitz, Kathy Montgomery and Jeff Chester, Linda Nussbaum, Ed Feinstein, and Gary Meisel.

Thanks to my family: Jim Eisenstock, Jay Eisenstock, Loretta Barrabee, Lorraine, Linda, Diane, Alan, Chris, Ben, and Nate.

Jonah, Kiva, and Randy, you make my day, every day.

Z, GG, and S, thank you forever.

Finally, thanks to Bobbie: LOML.

A final word: Over the months and months that Ron and I spoke, I carried a photo in my mind's eye that I still cannot shake. I see Ron walking down the center of a road. It could be West Florissant in Ferguson, or it could be a street in Baltimore, or Chicago, or Dallas, or New York, or Cleveland, or . . . sadly, any street in any city. Ron walks slowly but with purpose, and though he is surrounded on all sides by people, he walks alone. On one side, I see the residents of that city. On the other side, I see men and women in uniform. The faces of all these people are the same, their eyes expressing the same emotions: despair, anger, fear, frustration.

I look closer and I see tears welling up in Ron's eyes.

I know he wishes he could move out of the way and that law enforcement and citizens would walk down the same street together, toward the same goal, the same purpose, their faces all sharing another emotion: hope. That day may come. But right now, that day feels far away.

I want to acknowledge everyone on both sides. I learned from my dear friend Ron that we are not so different, we are not so far apart; we *can* come together. We just have to believe in each other.

DISCUSSION QUESTIONS

PROLOGUE: CONFRONTATION

In the prologue, Ron Johnson comes face-to-face with his own preconceived ideas about other people based on how they appear. What biases of your own do you need to acknowledge? How have your biases changed in recent years?

DAY 1: MICHAEL BROWN'S BODY

What was your initial reaction when you heard about the Michael Brown shooting in Ferguson? How did the reporting of that incident affect your perception of the police or of race relations in the US?

DAY 2: "THIS IS WAR"

What did you think when you heard about the rioting in Ferguson? How could the people and the police have responded differently?

DAY 3: "THESE PEOPLE"

What fears or biases are revealed in the trooper's use of the phrase "these people"? What can we do to move beyond seeing others as "these people" in order to find common ground for understanding each other?

DAY 4: "WHY AM I DIFFERENT?"

Describe your response to Ron's story about the time his father took him to jail. Do you think his father's actions were helpful? Harmful? Effective?

Describe a time when you felt different, hated, or misunderstood. How did you respond? Did it make you stronger or weaker? How did this event affect your faith in God?

DAY 5: WAITING FOR THE STORM

Ron's father-in-law tells him that the police need to do "something different" in response to the riots and unrest in Ferguson. What might they do differently that hasn't been tried yet?

Ron describes some confrontations between the police and journalists out on the street. What is the role of the mainstream media in shaping our understanding and perception of events such as those in Ferguson? What is the role of social media?

DAY 6 (DAYLIGHT): A DIFFERENT MORNING

Ron describes a valuable lifelong lesson he learned in boot camp with the Missouri State Highway Patrol: "It doesn't matter how strong you are physically. What matters is your inner strength. Your spirit. Your will. Your heart." Describe a time when your inner strength was tested or when it helped you accomplish a goal you had set for yourself.

DAY 6 (AFTER DARK): "I NEED ANSWERS"

What do you think of Ron's decision to march with the pro-testers? In what ways can we "march with" people who may oppose us or who differ from us? How can we become instruments of God's grace, mercy, and power in other people's lives?

DAY 7: "SAVE OUR SONS"

How does the release of the security camera video from the convenience store affect your perception of the Michael Brown shooting? Do you think it was the right decision to release the video to the public before turning it over to the grand jury? Why or why not?

In describing his preparation for one of his new conferences, Ron says, "I see myself as a police officer caught between the line of law enforcement I stand with and the people on the street—the citizens I've pledged to protect." Discuss your views on how the police should balance enforcing the law with serving the public.

DAY 8: "NO MORE THAN I CAN BEAR"

Sometimes, leadership means making decisions or doing things that are unpopular with the people we lead. How should leaders respond when they believe they are doing the right thing but others disagree?

DAY 9: "I AM YOU"

When Ron's boss tells him that public information officers will be taking over the news conferences and press interviews, Ron feels that they have taken away his voice. Have you had an experience in your life when you felt you lost your ability to speak for yourself or speak up for someone else? How did you respond? How did you get your voice back?

When Ron speaks at the memorial for Michael Brown, he apologizes to Michael Brown's family as a law enforcement officer, even though he was not responsible for Michael Brown's death. Do you think he did the right thing? Discuss the role of "representational repentance" in breaking down barriers between people.

DAY 10: A BULLET HAS NO NAME

Tension between law enforcement and the local community is at the heart of *13 Days in Ferguson*. Discuss practical ways in which members of local communities can work to improve relationships with law enforcement.

DAY 11: MAN, BLACK MAN, TROOPER

Ron observes that "faith is not what you feel. It's what you do." What is the role of faith in solving our differences with other people? If reconciliation is "a game of inches," discuss what you can do this week to make some incremental progress toward reconciliation with people who differ from you.

DAY 12: "WHERE HAVE YOU BEEN?"

Ron's strategy in Ferguson was to *walk, talk,* and *listen.* How can you apply this strategy in your local community to begin to foster positive change? What is the role of presence, persistence, and consistency in achieving positive results?

DAY 13: "TROUBLE DOESN'T LAST ALWAYS"

For change to take root and bear long-term fruit, we must teach succeeding generations the truths and values that undergird positive change. What can we do to teach our children how to get along better with people who are different from us?

EPILOGUE: AFTER FERGUSON

Ron advises us to "see people as people," "abandon labels," and "try not to prejudge." What can you do to begin to put his vision into practice? How hopeful are you that real change is possible?

ABOUT THE AUTHOR

CAPTAIN RONALD S. JOHNSON was born and raised in St. Louis, Missouri. He holds a criminal justice degree and is a graduate of Northwestern University Traffic Institute of Police Staff and Command and a 2014 graduate of the Federal Bureau of Investigation National Academy. He is certified in police instruction and the development and implementation of assessment-center exercises for command-level staff officers. Captain Johnson and his wife, Lori, have been married for twenty-nine years and have two adult children, Amanda and Bradley.

ALAN EISENSTOCK is the author of fifteen books, most recently *Hang Time: My Life in Basketball* (Houghton Mifflin Harcourt), written with NBA legend Elgin Baylor. He lives in Pacific Palisades, California.

THERE IS HOPE FOR HONEST AND HEALING CONVERSATION.

Get real about race with Benjamin Watson and the *Under Our Skin* experience.

Under Our Skin

After Ferguson, Benjamin Watson couldn't stay silent—and his comments took the Internet by storm. Now, in *Under Our Skin*, Watson honestly examines both sides of the race debate and appeals to the power and possibility of faith as a step toward healing.

Under Our Skin Group Conversation Guide

Based on the groundbreaking book *Under Our Skin*, this four-week guide for churches and small groups will foster honest conversation about race, bias, and justice in our nation.

CP1133